NEW IMAGES OF MAN

Published by The Museum of Modern Art, New York

in collaboration with The Baltimore Museum of Art

Distributed by Doubleday & Company, Inc., Garden City, New York

NEW

IMAGES

OF MAN

BY PETER SELZ   *with statements by the artists*

Published by the Museum of Modern Art, New York, 1959
All rights reserved
Library of Congress Catalogue Card Number 59-14221
Typography by Susan Draper
Cover design by Herbert Matter
Printed in Holland by Joh. Enschedé en Zonen, Haarlem

LENDERS TO THE EXHIBITION

Richard Brown Baker, New York; Leonard Baskin, Northampton, Massachusetts; Dr. and Mrs. Malcolm W. Bick, Springfield, Massachusetts; Mr. and Mrs. Sidney F. Brody, Los Angeles; Mr. and Mrs. William A. M. Burden, New York; Mr. and Mrs. Leo Castelli, New York; Mr. and Mrs. Ralph F. Colin, New York; Mr. and Mrs. Richard Deutsch, Greenwich, Connecticut; Philippe Dotremont, Brussels; Robert Elkon, New York; Mrs. Herbert S. Greenwald, Chicago; Dr. and Mrs. Julius S. Held, New York; Mr. and Mrs. Maxime L. Hermanos, New York; Joseph H. Hirshhorn, New York; Sterling Holloway, Encino, California; Mrs. Martha Jackson, New York; Philip C. Johnson, New Canaan, Connecticut; Mr. and Mrs. Harold Kaye, Great Neck, New York; Rico Lebrun, Los Angeles; Harold W. Lipman, New York; Mr. and Mrs. Albert A. List, New York; Mrs. H. Gates Lloyd, Washington, D. C.; Wright Ludington, Santa Barbara; Mr. and Mrs. Lewis Maniłow, Chicago; Mr. and Mrs. Arnold H. Maremont, Winnetka, Illinois; Mr. and Mrs. Pierre Matisse, New York; Mrs. Jan Muller, New York; Mr. and Mrs. Roy R. Neuberger, New York; Arthur J. Neumann, Chicago; Robert W. Ossorio, New York; Dr. and Mrs. Russel H. Patterson, Jr., New York; Mr. and Mrs. Walter Ross, New York; Mr. and Mrs. R. J. Sainsbury, London; Mr. and Mrs. Joseph R. Shapiro, Oak Park, Illinois; Mr. and Mrs. James Thrall Soby, New Canaan, Connecticut; Mr. and Mrs. Richard K. Weil, St. Louis; Mr. and Mrs. Joseph Weinstein, New York; Mr. and Mrs. Charles Zadok, New York; Mr. and Mrs. William Zeckendorf, Jr., New York.

Institute of Contemporary Art, Boston; Albright Art Gallery, Buffalo; The Art Institute of Chicago; Stedelijk van Abbe Museum, Eindhoven, The Netherlands; Department of Art, The Woman's College of the University of North Carolina, Greensboro; The Tate Gallery, London; Walker Art Center, Minneapolis; The Museum of Modern Art, New York; Whitney Museum of American Art, New York; Phoenix Art Museum, Arizona; Phillips Collection, Washington, D. C.

Galerie Creuzevault, Paris; Fine Arts Associates, New York; Allan Frumkin Gallery, Chicago; The Hanover Gallery, London; Martha Jackson Gallery, New York; Pierre Matisse Gallery, New York; Betty Parsons Gallery, New York; Frank Perls Gallery, Beverly Hills; Bertha Schaefer Gallery, New York; Jacques Seligmann & Co., Inc., New York.

ACKNOWLEDGMENTS

On behalf of the Trustees of The Museum of Modern Art and The Baltimore Museum of Art, I wish first to express my gratitude to the artists for their gracious collaboration in providing the texts in this book, as well as invaluable documentation about their work, and to the generous lenders to the exhibition on which this book is based, whose names appear on page 5.

I want to thank Alicia Legg, Assistant Curator of the Department of Painting and Sculpture Exhibitions, for her able and resourceful work in helping to assemble the material for the exhibition. In addition, I owe gratitude to Miss Legg, Dr. Ilse Falk, Research Assistant of the Department, and to my wife Thalia Selz for research, editorial assistance and help in translations. Dr. Falk, with the assistance of Bernard Karpel, also prepared the bibliography. I wish especially to thank Karen Bokert for her efficient secretarial help in both exhibition and book.

Frank O'Hara wrote the essay on Jackson Pollock.

For special assistance given us, our deepest thanks are due to: Mr. Charles Alan; The Institute of Contemporary Art, Boston; Mr. Joseph H. Hirshhorn; Mr. Sterling Holloway; Mr. and Mrs. Lewis Manilow; Mr. and Mrs. Pierre Matisse; Mr. and Mrs. Roy R. Neuberger; Mr. Jacques Seligmann.

I am deeply grateful to René d'Harnoncourt, Director of the Museum, for the brilliant installation of the exhibition.

Peter Selz
Director of the Exhibition

CONTENTS

El sueño de la razón produce monstruos   GOYA

A PREFATORY NOTE BY PAUL TILLICH

Each period has its peculiar image of man. It appears in its poems and novels, music, philosophy, plays and dances; and it appears in its painting and sculpture. Whenever a new period is conceived in the womb of the preceding period, a new image of man pushes towards the surface and finally breaks through to find its artists and philosophers. We have been living for decades at a turning point, and nothing is more indicative of this fact than the series of revolutionary styles in the visual arts which have followed each other since the beginning of our century. Each of these styles transformed the image of man drastically, even when compared to the changes of the past five centuries. Where are the organic forms of man's body, the human character of his face, the uniqueness of his individual person? And finally, when in abstract or non-objective painting and sculpture, the figure disappears completely, one is tempted to ask, what has happened to man? This is the question which we direct at our contemporary artists, and in this question one can discern an undertone of embarassment, of anger and even of hostility against them. Instead, we should ask ourselves, what has become of us? What has happened to the reality of our lives? If we listen to the more profound observers of our period, we hear them speak of the danger in which modern man lives: the danger of losing his humanity and of becoming a thing amongst the things he produces. Humanity is not something man simply has. He must fight for it anew in every generation, and he may lose his fight. There have been few periods in history in which a catastrophic defeat was more threatening than in ours. One need only look at the dehumanizing structure of the totalitarian systems in one half of the world, and the dehumanizing consequences of technical mass civilization in the other half. In addition, the conflict between them may lead to the annihilation of humanity. The impact of this predicament produces, on the one hand, adaptation to the necessities of present-day living and indifference to the question of the meaning of human existence, and on the other, anxiety, despair and revolt against this predicament. The first group resigns itself to becoming things amongst things, giving up its individual self. The second group tries desparately to resist this danger.

The works of art of our century are the mirrors of our predicament produced by some of the most sensitive minds of our time. In the light of our predicament we must look at the works of contemporary art, and conversely, in the light of contemporary works of art we must look at our predicament.

The image of man became transformed, distorted, disrupted and it finally disappeared in recent art. But as in the reality of our lives, so in its mirror of the visual arts, the human protest arose against the fate to become a thing. The artists, who are shown in this exhibition, are representatives of such protest. They want to regain the image of man in their paintings and sculptures, but they are too honest to turn back to earlier naturalistic or idealistic forms, and they are too conscious of the limits implied in our present situation to jump ahead into a so-called new classicism. They tried to depict as honestly as they could, true representations of the human predicament, as they experienced it within and outside themselves. The question as to how well they succeeded artistically cannot be answered by the present writer. It is a matter of art criticism. But the question as to how well they succeeded in stating the content of their works is a matter of personal and philosophical interpretation.

The fight for a full development of man's possibilities is a continuous task. It is never completely reached and will never be completely missed. But in some moments of history as expressed in the mosaics of Ravenna, in Giotto, in Piero della Francesa, in Manet, more fulfillment is visible than in other moments. And at certain times and with certain artists—early Romanesque, late Gothic, Breughel, Bosch, El Greco, Magnasco, Goya and Daumier—the pain of struggle is more visible. But neither the fulfillment nor the struggle determines the artistic quality of the work. And something else must be added here: the very fact that a great work of art depicts the negative side in the fight for humanity is in itself a fulfillment of a high human possibility. The courage and the honesty which underlie such works, and the creative power which is able to grasp the negativity of the content by the positivity of the form, is a triumph of humanity.

In the development of art since the beginning of our century the negative emphasis in the expression of the fight for humanity by far prevails. This is also true of the works presented in this exhibition with their distortions. All of them show traces of the battle for the human image they want to rediscover. They resist the temptation of tired relapses or premature solutions. They fight desparately over the image of man, and by producing shock and fascination in the observer, they communicate their own concern for threatened and struggling humanity. They show the smallness of man and his deep involvement in the vast masses of inorganic matter out of which he tries to emerge with toil and pain; they demonstrate the controlling power of technical forms over man by dissecting him into parts and re-constructing him, as man does with nature. They reveal the hidden presence of animal trends in the unconscious and the primitive mass-man from which man comes and to which civilized mass-man may return. They dare to emphasize certain elements and parts of the natural figure and to leave out others in the desire to express something which nature hides. And if they depict the human face, they show that it is not simply given to us but that its human form itself is a matter of continuous struggle. There are demonic forces in every man which try to take possession of him, and the new image of man shows faces in which the state of being possessed is shockingly manifest. In others the fear of such possession or the anxiety at the thought of living is predominant, and again in others there are feelings of emptiness, meaninglessness and despair. But there are also courage, longing and hope, a reaching out into the unknown.

INTRODUCTION

Marsyas had no business playing the flute. Athena, who invented it, had tossed it aside because it distorted the features of the player. But when Marsyas, the satyr of Phrygia, found it, he discovered that he could play on it the most wondrous strains. He challenged beautiful Apollo, who then calmly played the strings of his lyre and won the contest. Apollo's victory was almost complete, and his divine proportions, conforming to the measures of mathematics, were exalted in fifth-century Athens and have set the standard for the tradition of Western art. But always there was the undercurrent of Marsyas' beauty struggling past the twisted grimaces of a satyr. These strains have their measure not in the rational world of geometry but in the depth of man's emotion. Instead of a canon of ideal proportions we are confronted by what Nietzsche called "the eternal wounds of existence." Among the artists who come to mind are the sculptors of the Age of Constantine, of Moissac and Souillac, the painters of the Book of Durrow, the Beatus Manuscripts, and the Campo Santo; Hieronymus Bosch, Grünewald, Goya, Picasso and Beckmann.

Again in this generation a number of painters and sculptors, courageously aware of a time of dread, have found articulate expression for the "wounds of existence." This voice may "dance and yell like a madman" (Jean Dubuffet), like the drunken, flute-playing maenads of Phrygia.

The revelations and complexities of mid-twentieth-century life have called forth a profound feeling of solitude and anxiety. The imagery of man which has evolved from this reveals sometimes a new dignity, sometimes despair, but always the uniqueness of man as he confronts his fate. Like Kierkegaard, Heidegger, Camus, these artists are aware of anguish and dread, of life in which man—precarious and vulnerable—confronts the precipice, is aware of dying as well as living.

Their response is often deeply human without making use of recognizable human imagery. It is found, for instance, in Mark Rothko's expansive ominous surfaces of silent contemplation, or in Jackson Pollock's wildly intensive act of vociferous affirmation with its total commitment by the artist. In the case of the painters and sculptors discussed here, however, a new human imagery unique to our century has been evolved.

Like the more abstract artists of the period, these imagists take the human situation, indeed the human predicament rather than formal structure, as their starting point. Existence rather than essence is of the greatest concern to them.

11

And if Apollo, from the pediment of Olympia to Brancusi's *Torso of a Young Man*, represents essence, the face of Marsyas has the dread of existence, the premonition of being flayed alive.

These images do not indicate the "return to the human figure" or the "new humanism" which the advocates of the academies have longed for, which, indeed they and their social-realist counterparts have hopefully proclaimed with great frequency, ever since the rule of the academy was shattered. There is surely no sentimental revival and no cheap self-aggrandizement in these effigies of the disquiet man.

These images are often frightening in their anguish. They are created by artists who are no longer satisfied with "significant form" or even the boldest act of artistic expression. They are perhaps aware of the mechanized barbarism of a time which, notwithstanding Buchenwald and Hiroshima, is engaged in the preparation of even greater violence in which the globe is to be the target. Or perhaps they express their rebellion against a dehumanization in which man, it seems, is to be reduced to an object of experiment. Some of these artists have what Paul Tillich calls the "courage to be," to face the situation and to state the absurdity. "Only the cry of anguish can bring us to life."[1]

But politics, philosophy and morality do not in themselves account for their desire to formulate these images. The act of showing forth these effigies takes the place of politics and moral philosophy, and the showing forth must stand in its own right as artistic creation.

In many ways these artists are inheritors of the romantic tradition. The passion, the emotion, the break with both idealistic form and realistic matter, the trend towards the demoniac and cruel, the fantastic and imaginary—all belong to the romantic movement which, beginning in the eighteenth century, seems never to have stopped.

But the art historian can also relate these images to the twentieth-century tradition. Although most of the works show no apparent debt to cubism, they would be impossible without the cubist revolution in body image and in pictorial space. Apollinaire tells us in his allegorical language that one of Picasso's friends "brought him one day to the border of a mystical country whose inhabitants were at once so simple and so grotesque that one could easily remake them. And then after all, since anatomy, for instance, no longer existed in art, he had to reinvent it, and carry out his own assassination with the practised and methodical hand of a great surgeon."[2] Picasso's reinvention of anatomy, which has been called cubism, was primarily concerned with exploring the *reality of form* and its relation to space, whereas the imagists we are now dealing with

Picasso: *"Ma Jolie" (Won a Zither or Guitar)*. (19 Oil on canvas, 39¾ × 25¾ Museum of Modern Ar York, acquired through th P. Bliss Bequest

often tend to use a similarly shallow space in which they explore the *reality of man*. In a like fashion the unrestricted use of materials by such artists as Dubuffet and Paolozzi would have been impossible without the early collages by Picasso and Braque, but again the cubists were playing with reality for largely formal reasons, whereas the contemporary artists may use pastes, cinder, burlap or nails to reinforce their psychological presentation.

These men own a great debt to the emotionally urgent and subjectively penetrating painting of the expressionists from the early Kokoschka to the late Soutine. Like them they renounce *la belle peinture* and are "bored by the esthetic," as Dubuffet writes. Like most expressionists these artists convey an almost mystical faith in the power of the effigy, to the making of which they are driven by "inner necessity." Yet the difference lies in this special power of the effigy, which has become an icon, a poppet, a fetish. Kokoschka and Soutine still do likenesses, no matter how preoccupied with their own private agonies and visions; Dubuffet and de Kooning depart further from specificity, and present us with a more generalized concept of Man or Woman.

Much of this work would be inconceivable without Dada's audacious break with the sacrosanct "rules of art" in favor of free self-contradiction, but negativism, shock value, and polemic are no longer ends in themselves. The surrealists, too, used the devices of Dada—the rags, the pastes, the ready-mades, the found object—and transported the picture into the realm of the fantastic and supernatural. Here the canvas becomes a magic object. Non-rational subjects are treated spontaneously, semi-automatically, sometimes deliriously. Dream, hallucination and confusion are used in a desire "to deepen the foundations of the real." Automatism was considered both a satisfying and powerful means of expression because it took the artist to the very depths of his being. The con-

Kokoschka: *Hans Tietze and Erica Tietze-Conrat*. (1909). Oil on canvas, 30¼ 53⅜". The Museum of Modern Art, New York, Mrs. John D. Rockefeller, Jr. Fund

Giacometti: *The Palace at 4 A.M.* (1932-33). Construction in wood, glass, wire, string, 25″ high. The Museum of Modern Art, New York. Purchase

scious was to be visibly linked to the unconscious and fused into a mysterious whole as in Giacometti's *The Palace at 4 A.M.*, where the reference of each object within the peculiarly shifting space—the space of the dream—is so ambiguous as never to furnish a precise answer to our question about it. But all too often surrealism "offered us only a subject when we needed an image."[3] The surrealist artist wants us to inquire, to attempt to "read" the work, and to remain perplexed. In the *City Square* (page 71), which Giacometti did sixteen years later, we are no longer dealing with a surrealist object. The space still isolates the figures, but instead of an ambiguous dream image we have a more specific statement about man's lack of mutual relationship.

Finally the direct approach to the material itself on the part of contemporary painters and sculptors, the concern with color as pigment, the interest in the surface as a surface, belongs to these artists as much as it does to the non-figurative painters and sculptors of our time. The material—the heavy pigmentation in de Kooning's "Women," the corroded surfaces of Richier's sculpture—help indeed in conveying the meaning. Dubuffet was one of the first artists who granted almost complete autonomy to his material when he did his famous "pastes" of the early 1940s. Even Francis Bacon wrote: "Painting in this sense tends towards a complete interlocking of image and paint, so that the image is in the paint and vice versa... I think that painting today is pure intuition and luck and taking advantage of what happens when you splash the stuff down."[4] But it is also important to remember that Dubuffet's or Bacon's forms never simply emerge from an undifferentiated id. These artists never abdicate their control of form.

14

The painters and sculptors discussed here have been open to a great many influences, have indeed sought to find affirmation in the art of the past. In addition to the art of this century—Picasso, Gonzales, Miró, Klee, Nolde, Soutine, etc.—they have learned to know primarily the arts of the non-Renaissance tradition: children's art, latrine art, and what Dubuffet calls *art brut*;[5] the sculpture of the early Etruscans and the late Romans, the Aztecs, and Neolithic cultures. When these artist look to the past, it is the early and late civilizations which captivate them. And when they study an African carving, they are enraptured not so much by its plastic quality or its tactile values, but rather by its presence as a totemic image. They may appreciate the ancient tribal artist's formal sensibilities; they truly *envy* his shamanistic powers.

The artists represented here—painters and sculptors, European and American—have arrived at a highly interesting and perhaps significant imagery which is concomitant with their formal structures. This combination of contemporary form with a new kind of iconography developing into a "New Image" is the only element these artists hold in common. It cannot be emphasized too strongly that this is not a school, not a group, not a movement. In fact, few of these artists know each other and any similarities are the result of the time in which they live and see. They are individuals affirming their personal identity as artists in a time of stereotypes and standardizations which have affected not only life in general but also many of our contemporary art exhibitions. Because of the limitations of space, we could not include many artists whose work merits recognition. While it is hoped that the selection proves to be wise, it must also be said that it was the personal choice of the director of the exhibition.

KAREL APPEL · born 1921

Painting is a tangible sensual experience, an intense state of emotion engendered by the joys and tragedies of man and also an experience in space which, fed by the instinct, leads to a living form. This atmosphere in which I breathe and which I make tangible through paint is an expression of my time. I try to catch this concrete reality with the means at my disposal. — *1950*

My paint tube is like a rocket which describes its own space. I try to make the impossible possible. What is happening I cannot foresee; it is a surprise. Painting, like passion, is an emotion full of truth and rings a living sound, like the roar coming from the lion's breast. — *1956*

It is feeling that directs the ordering process on the white canvas. The unused white ground is magnificent. It makes manifest all spontaneous handling and accidents, as well as the lines, directly and spontaneously applied, which thus change to a more profound matter. — *1957*

To paint is to destroy what preceded. I never try to make a painting, but a chunk of life. It is a scream; it is a night; it is like a child; it is a tiger behind bars.

Most of our contemporaries have not yet grown beyond the "being" of things as we have known them and they are still tied to folkloristic miniature concepts expressed in poetical form and color. The new poetic idea is a free expression, comparable to modern science which has found free energy, that is, liberation from the gravitational force of the earth. — *1958*

Karel Appel, from letters, translated from the Dutch by Ernst Scheyer, Detroit

The young Dutch artists who formed the Experimental Group in Amsterdam in 1948 rejected not only the moribund academies, but just as much the painting of Mondrian and de Stijl. Mondrian's painting had not brought about the better co-operative society he had envisaged, nor did it seem likely to do so in the future. Appel, Corneille and Constant, who formed the Group, wished to go back to the primeval sources of man's creative expression.

Their iconography, which often equated man and animal, is related to the work of the Belgian expressionists of the School of Laethem St. Martin in the inter-war period. The painting of Constant Permeke and Frits van den Berghe

Appel: *Person in Grey*. 1953. Oil on canvas, 46 × 35″.
Martha Jackson Gallery, New York

is especially relevant to this context. But this iconography may actually have
had its immediate source in the work of Heinrich Campendonk who taught at
the Rijksakademie in Amsterdam from 1933 to 1957 after having been one of
the original members of the Blue Rider and a close friend of Franz Marc. It
was Campendonk who continued Marc's attempt to find formal expression for
man's identification with the animal in a total cosmic union. Appel, indeed,
had studied at the Rijksakademie from 1940 to 1943, but his man-animal
iconography is expressed with a new, turbulent vigor, which makes the older
expressionists appear lyrical, even mild, by comparison.

Soon Appel and his friends made contact with similar groups in Copenhagen and Brussels, and the group COBRA (for Copenhagen—Brussels—Amsterdam) resulted in 1949. The magazine of the same name was devoted to primitive, folk, schizophrenic and child art, and to startling comparisons of a surreal nature. But COBRA declared itself as much opposed to "surrealist pessimism" as to "sterile abstraction" and "bourgeois naturalism." They affirmed their optimism and, much like the New York painters of the late Forties, they believed in the "act of creation" as the all-important aspect of the esthetic experience. "I never try to make a painting, but a chunk of life. It is a scream; it is a night; it is like a child; it is a tiger behind bars."

The same year as the foundation of COBRA, Appel painted a fresco for the coffee shop in the City Hall of Amsterdam which aroused so much controversy that it was covered over with wallpaper, and shortly thereafter, in 1950, Appel moved to Paris where he is still living. He began to participate in Michel Tapié's exhibitions, "Signifiants de l'Informel" (1951) and "Un Art Autre" (1952) and soon began showing at the Internationals of Pittsburgh (1952, 1955, 1959), São Paulo (1953), and Venice (1954). He now has murals in the Stedelijk Museum in Amsterdam and at the Unesco Building in Paris among other places.

In his murals as well as in his easel painting, Appel has been able to sustain the urgency and fervor of his early work. A canvas such as *Person in Grey* of 1953 (page 17) departs from the close resemblance to children's drawings. He has clearly learned from Klee, but this is Klee gone violent, almost berserk. Klee's paintings look like subtle and sophisticated miniatures next to Appel's work. *The Condemned* (page 19) of the same year, adds a note of black nightmare—the "tiger behind bars."

Appel is one of the few inventive portrait painters of our time. His portraits combine his peculiar expressionism with the new concern for the act of painting itself. *Portrait of Sandberg* (page 21), for instance, is impetuously built up of zigzag calligraphic strokes and heavy impasto. It is a likeness which retains the dynamic events of the creative process. The brilliantly colored *Count Basie* (page 20), one of a series of jazz musicians Appel painted during his stay in the United States in 1957, is likewise related to the spontaneity of action painting. Clearly a parallel can be drawn between his improvisations and the technique of jazz.

Appel's recent work, such as the large 1957 *Blue Nude* (page 22), with its continuous movement in the picture plane, becomes even more intoxicated with the sensual quality of color and paint. Out of the maelstrom of experience the streaked pigment forms the grotesque image of a woman.

Appel: *The Condemned.* 1953. Oil on canvas, 55¾ × 45¼". Stedelijk van Abbe Museum, Eindhoven, The Netherlands

Appel: *Count Basie*. 1957. Oil on canvas, 60 x 45". Phoenix Art Museum, gift of Peter Rübel

Appel: *Portrait of Sandberg*. 1956. Oil on canvas, 51¼ × 31⅞". Institute of Contemporary Art, Boston, Provisional Collection through Mr. and Mrs. Lester H. Dana

Appel: *Blue Nude.* 1957. Oil on canvas, 76¾ × 51¼". Collection Philippe Dotremont, Brussels

KENNETH ARMITAGE   born 1916

The artist is concerned with expressing the most he can with the tightest economy, containing the comprehension of a wider experience in an isolated single fragment, reducing an awareness of all time to the single moment.

An essential requirement of sculpture is that it must present an easily recognizable over-all pattern or envelope, a simple total image which is first a basket and only secondly holds the eggs.

However one might change its character, the single figure remains a unit shape deeply satisfying in itself. But if three or four figures are placed together (and I always wanted to make groups or crowds) an over-all shape cannot be achieved just by neatly arranging the unchanged units inside it for this would look elaborate and contrived. Joining figures together in groups, I found in time I wanted to merge them so completely they formed a new organic unit — a simple mass of whatever shape I liked containing only that number of heads, limbs or other detail I felt necessary. So in a crowd we see only the face or hand that catches our eye, for we don't see mathematically but only what is most conspicuous or important or familiar.

Abstract sculpture, or sculpture concerning subjects other than the human image cannot hold my interest for long — it is too polite, like people who are too shy ever to take off their clothes.

A sculptor using figures reveals a little of his private human self as well as his aesthetic inclinations. We are all involved in ceaseless and ruthless scrutiny of others, and become adept in making automatic split-second assessments of everybody we meet — being repelled or attracted, and interpreting every variation of shape as indications of character.

Naturally my sculpture contains ideas or experiences other than those that derive directly from observation of the human image, nevertheless it is always dressed in some degree in human form.

Kenneth Armitage

Sculpture in England has experienced an extraordinary renaissance—birth would be a more accurate description—during the last thirty years. Between the wars Henry Moore and Barbara Hepworth, exploiting the nature of materials as well as the essence of archetypal forms, set a standard of quality which more recent sculptors have continued. Of the triumvirate—Butler, Chadwick and Armitage—who came to public attention around 1950, Kenneth Armitage is the youngest.

Armitage was born in Leeds in 1916 and studied at the Leeds College of Art from 1934 to 1937 before going down to London where he attended the Slade School from 1937 until 1939. He first became prominent in 1952 with a one-man show at Gimpel Fils and participation in the Venice Biennale. In 1954 Bertha Schaefer introduced him to the United States.

Armitage's recent sculpture continues his concern with the simplified human figure, alone or in groups. He works in the pliable clay medium and then finishes the bronze surfaces by filling, scratching, or gouging, and sometimes by applying color, but the final sensuous texture relates very closely to the form itself. Very recent works such as *Model for Large Seated Group* and *Diarchy*, both of 1957 (below and opposite), remind us of his earlier slab-like compositions. Again he presents a collective group merged into a continuous screen which is not true sculpture-in-the-round and needs to be seen from the front. But the nervously moving and still slightly contrived webs of the early Fifties have made way for a compact slab, a frieze, indeed a wall, animated only by the pointed

eft: Armitage: *Model for Large Seated Group.*
). Bronze, 10″ high. Collection Mr. and
Maxime L. Hermanos, New York

Armitage: *Model for Krefeld Monument.*
). Bronze, 13¼″ high. Collection Mr. and
Walter Ross, New York

tage: *Diarchy.* (1957). Bronze, 68¼″ high.
ction Mr. and Mrs. Arnold H. Maremont,
etka, Illinois

25

Left: Armitage: *Seated Woman with Arms Raised*. (1953-57). Bronze, 41½″ high. Albright Art Gallery, Buffalo, gift of Seymour H. Knox

Right: Armitage: *The Seasons*. (1956). Bronze, 34″ high. Collection Mr. and Mrs. Charles Zadok, New York

breasts and spider-like legs sprouting out from the surface and by the skyline of squared-off head-shapes. Related to Moore's *Family Group* of 1945-49, these are far more anonymous and impersonal clusters of sitters, merged together inextricably into a single unit. The very concept—the impressive stolidity of a group—seems to have grown into its shape during the modeling process and is due to the artist's desire to "achieve area without actual bulk."[6]

The group for the war monument, to be erected in Krefeld, Germany, breaks up Armitage's solidity and exists freely in the surrounding space, indeed commands the environment. Surfaces, reminiscent of Rodin and Medardo Rosso, enrich these moving figures. Without massiveness the group is monumental, that is, it does not put us at ease, but admonishes and mystifies us.

In *The Seasons* (opposite) Armitage combines the linear forms of modern sculpture with a traditional respect for solidity. Torsos perch on thin legs, like a modern building on stilts. The vertical emphasis of the organ-pipe legs is continued in the triple accent of arms reaching up ceremoniously like standards waiting for banners, while the out-stretched horizontal arm sets up a minor axis.

His individual figures, such as *Seated Woman with Arms Raised* (opposite), are large helpless creatures, thwarted by the inflexible limbs which keep them from assuming control of their environment. Like Gregor in Kafka's *Metamorphosis*, these human figures with their thin extremities are turned into helpless bugs; "...they signify nothing more than the absurdity of the body that the human spirit is condemned to occupy."[7]

Bacon: *Study of a Figure in a*
(1952). Oil on canvas,
Phillips Collection, Washin

FRANCIS BACON   born 1910

Francis Bacon, like Joyce, was born in Dublin and the excrutiatingly painful horror of Bacon's imagery recalls Father Arnall's sermon on the terrors of hell in *A Portrait of the Artist as a Young Man*. Bacon's figures, howling with torture and guilt, suggest the physical and spiritual pain of the damned on which the Jesuit father perorates. Bacon's earliest paintings, in fact, were studies on the theme of the Crucifixion—strangely distorted and deformed monsters combining features of birds, pigs, bats and humans: modern versions of Bosch. Later works such as the interpretation of Velasquez' *Pope Innocent X* of 1953 (page 30), are shrieking accusations, combining an anti-clerical with an anti-art attitude. Here is the Pope on the macabre stage of the Grand Guignol.

Bacon's figures are both haunted and haunting. Like surrealist figures, the sombre *Man in a Blue Box* (page 31), is taken out of time and out of place as he emits a cry which touches us at the base of the spine. This is anguish and violence, observed and recorded. While the surrealists might have thought of placing a man in a transparent box, and the expressionists of distorting his features, Bacon has affirmed his horror by cruelly unhinging his features. This man suggests a weird judge pronouncing punishment on himself, an imprisonment which has already taken place. He recalls also the character of Hamm in Samuel Becket's *Endgame* who throughout the long dialogue, speaking through the sheet with which he is covered, pleads for his pain-killer. When at last the time for the pain-killer has come he is told: "there is no more pain-killer."

Man in a Blue Box was done in 1949, the year of Bacon's first one-man exhibition at the Hanover Gallery in London, at which time he came to critical attention for his preoccupation with horror. The fearful isolation of his subjects, their raw estrangement from the world, is brought to a high pitch again in *Study of a Figure in a Landscape* of 1952 (page 28). Applications of blues and greens, so spare that the unsized canvas is seen in many areas, suggest a field of grass against woods and sky. In the dark center, the only opaque part of the picture, crouches a figure which seems to have all of man's explosive force. Like so many of Bacon's images, it is out of focus. Bacon is interested in motion studies, in the film and in the flash-light news photographs of crime and accident. By transferring the motion of the film onto canvas he sometimes achieves the sequential quality of time, motion and action.[8] But in addition to physical motion, he is also interested in psychological motivations. His image of man is blurred, as man's memory is blurred.

In these sparsely painted works the texture of the canvas has determined the

Bacon: *Study after Velasquez' Portrait of Pope Innocent X.* (1953). Oil on canvas, 60½ × 46½". Collection Mr. and Mrs. William A. M. Burden, New York

texture of the finished work. In recent years, however, he has become interested in brighter colors and richer application of the pigment, as in the van Gogh studies. Here, as in the series after Velasquez, his imagination is sparked by an earlier work of art. In the 1956 study (page 32) van Gogh materializes in the fields together with a shadow from which he seems quite detached. Emerging

out of the quickly receding space, he reminds us that time is on its way. In a
later study (page 33) he has stopped on the road. Always concerned with the
vision of death and man's consciousness of dying, Bacon has presented us here
with the spectre of van Gogh returning from the dead to his familiar haunts on
the road to Tarascon.[9]

Bacon: *Study for Portrait of van Gogh, No. 1.* (1956). Oil on canvas, 60 × 46½".
Collection Mr. and Mrs. R. J. Sainsbury, London

Bacon: *Study for Portrait of van Gogh, No. 3.* (1957). Oil on
78¼ × 56¼". Collection Joseph H. Hirshhorn, New York

33

Baskin: *Man with a Dead Bird*. (1954). Walnut, 64″
high. The Museum of Modern Art, New York,
A. Conger Goodyear Fund

34

LEONARD BASKIN born 1922

...Our human frame, our gutted mansion, our enveloping sack of beef and ash is yet a glory. Glorious in defining our universal sodality and glorious in defining our utter uniqueness. The human figure is the image of all men and of one man. It contains all and it can express all. Man has always created the human figure in his own image, and in our time that image is despoiled and debauched. Between eye and eye stretches an interminable landscape. From pelvis to sternum lies the terror of great structures, and from arms to ankle to the center of the brain is a whirling axis. To discover these marvels, to search the maze of man's physicality, to wander the body's magnitudes is to search for the image of man. And in the act of discovery lies the act of communication. A common communal communication of necessity.

The forging of works of art is one of man's remaining semblances to divinity. Man has been incapable of love, wanting in charity and despairing of hope. He has not molded a life of abundance and peace, and he has charted the earth and befouled the heavens more wantonly than ever before. He has made of Arden a landscape of death. In this garden I dwell, and in limning the horror, the degradation and the filth, I hold the cracked mirror up to man. All previous art makes this course inevitable.

Leonard Baskin, Northampton, Mass., April 23, 1959

In vehement opposition to what he calls "the subjective ambiguities" of a great deal of contemporary art, Baskin feels that the artist is, above all, a communicator of moral ideas. "Avant-garde art," he writes in his recent essay on Käthe Kolwitz, "is not complex, indeed it is simple minded," because it replaces specific content with "the formal substructure."[10]

In order to communicate, Leonard Baskin makes use of the print medium in woodcuts and wood engravings and does fine limited editions of books for the Gehenna Press. As a member of the Smith College faculty, he has been an inspiring teacher for a number of years. But it is in his sculpture that he has found his most consummate expression.

Like Francis Bacon, Baskin is preoccupied with the state of death and the act of dying. His prints and drawings, with their incisive, web-like line, dwell on the ravaged image of man perishing of his own physical defilement and spiritual corruption.

Baskin: *Poet Laureate*. (1956). Bronze, 9″ high. Collection Mr. and Mrs. Roy R. Neuberger, New York

A similar interpretation appears in the small bronzes, whose corrosion resembles the weathered textures of archaic works. The *Seated Man* (page 38) is actually a funny little fellow, pig-eyed and neckless, his large arms folded, tiny legs hanging down from a heavy belly. But a more macabre humor has surmounted the bloated, heavy-jowled, degenerate face of the *Poet Laureate* (above) with a laurel wreath: a would-be Caesar uttering absurdities.

His carvings in wood and stone, however, are no longer representations of agony and deterioration. Here man assumes a quiet, dignified nobility. Symmetrical and frontal, silent and static—even the *Walking Man* (page 38) is a static figure—they have an almost iconic intensity and self-containment. Unlike almost all of his contemporaries, Baskin, who has great reverence for the past, disdains open forms and space extensions. Rather than form governing space, Baskin's image, as in the *Man with a Dead Bird* (page 34), dominates the viewer,

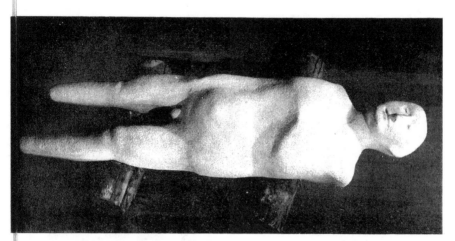

Baskin: *The Great Dead Man.* (1956). Limestone, 5' 10" long. Owned by the artist

who is captivated by the compelling severity of the simplified form and the inscrutable expression.

Baskin's sculpture has been exhibited since 1939, but his most important work to date is the *Great Dead Man* of 1956 (above). One of an extensive series of effigies of the dead in bronze, stone, and wood—it is a massive limestone figure, stiffly frontal, its solid rigidity expressing the very essence of rigor mortis. Compared to this, the medieval tomb sculptures which impressed him during his studies at the Académie de la Grande Chaumière in Paris in 1950 and at the Academy of Fine Arts in Florence in 1951, look fragile and linear. We must go back to the Old Kingdom sculpture of Egypt to find the true source of Baskin's monoliths, and perhaps also—if we observe the secret smile of final renunciation on the lips of the *Great Dead Man*—to certain Buddhist effigies of the Northern Wei dynasty in fifth-century China.

37

Left: Baskin: *Walking Man.* (1955). Oak, 17¼" high. Collection Dr. and Mrs. Malcolm W. Bick, Springfield, Massachusetts

Right: Baskin: *Seated Man.* (1956). Bronze, 13½" high. Collection Dr. and Mrs. Julius S. Held, New York

REG BUTLER   born 1913

...*ignorance, incompleteness and misrepresentation must always be the natural bedfellows of the artist involved in attempting a directly figurative image... doing small things well is admirable and appropriate in science and technology because their achievements are cumulative; but it is not the same in the arts... to achieve anything worthwhile they must always be prepared to afford the unfashionable luxury of failure...*

...*somewhere at the back of my mind I think there has always been a conviction that to achieve an appropriate paraphrase of his own image may well be the most considerable achievement of which man will ever be capable... even perhaps a feeling that a society which evades a resolution of its own face may in the course of time be seen to have failed itself in a thousand other respects...*

...*if what is natural is of any significance, figuration is natural to sculpture... the sculptor is an organiser of forms before all else just as contrariwise the painter is an organiser of marks, and as the painter's natural preoccupation leads, it seems to me, towards landscape (it is as landscape that I see the majority of the works I find most admirable in present-day painting) so the sculptor's attachment to object-making leads naturally towards the creation of the "magic object," the personage, the creature, the human animal... it would appear that for very many sculptors today the figurative direction is an open one, while it is perhaps otherwise for many active and dedicated painters.*

...*the tensions of life today exist in the framework of an equally dynamic biological optimism... tautness has its greatest value when it is expressed through forms which are potentially capable of being relaxed... sculptures in which all is tension are as false as were the security sculptures of the nineteenth century.*

...*reality has usually little connection with literal accuracy... sometimes it is necessary to get the centre of energy up off the ground in order to anchor it... a fragment can be more whole than mere completeness, perhaps because it includes the element of event... it becomes a part of history rather than a scientific specimen in a glass case.*

...*gesture is to be found as much in the axes of forms as in the handling of surface... the mark of the artist goes all through whatever he makes.*

...*sculpture must involve feeling oneself into one's work, for the sculptor and his work share the same actual space and enjoy the same physical dimensions... the legs of the figure a sculptor makes carry actual weight. Its arms penetrate space and its mass is pulled down towards the centre of the earth just as he has to carry his own load.*

Reg Butler, from a conversation recorded in England in 1959

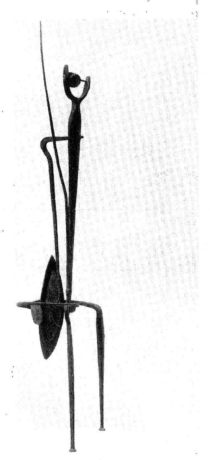

Butler: *Woman*. (1949). Forged iron,
7′ 3″ high. The Tate Gallery, London

If both Baskin and Bacon present man confronted with death, Reg Butler, especially in his recent work, presents life in its most sensual and erotic aspects as symbolized by woman. This aroused female demon, desirous and desirable, close to the earth, is part of that peculiar Western tradition born in the Korai of Greece and extending to Maillol and Lachaise.

But Butler's early work was totally different in derivation and in appearance. After training as an architect, Butler worked during the war as a blacksmith in a village in West Sussex. When he turned to sculpture in 1944, Butler began to weld iron bars into linear structures like sinewy limbs, allowing the forged farm implements to impose their own forms on his. Instead of beautifully weathered rocks, pebbles and wood, he used iron of great tensile strength. He had little respect for the natural appearance of his material and broke with the solid forms of Moore and Hepworth, beginning to draw in space with thin metal rods. In these early sculptures he may have been influenced by the welded sculpture of Julio Gonzalez and Picasso's surrealist drawings of fantastic anatomies. The resultant figures—and Butler's sculpture always relates to the human figure— also resemble bird and insect forms, or skeletal cages whose thorniness recalls the spiky rituals Graham Sutherland painted during the war.

Butler's first one-man show was at the Hanover Gallery in London in 1949. As early as 1951 he was receiving sculpture commissions in Great Britain. In 1953 Curt Valentin introduced him to America and in the same year he was awarded the grand prize in the international competition for a design for the monument to The Unknown Political Prisoner.

Butler's maquette was attacked by a biased press and by sculptors with vested interests in retrograde war monuments for being abstract and anti-humanistic. Yet this is a moving symbol of tyranny in our time. The sculpture (page 42), in the collection of the Museum of Modern Art, is a replica of the original model which was damaged by an ill-advised refugee artist during the exhibition at the Tate Gallery in London in 1953. In a description which accompanied the maquette, Butler explained that this, unlike the Cenotaph in London (or the Washington Monument), is not a purely abstract solution, but consists of "three elements: the *natural rock foundation* which provides a fundamentally 'natural' setting even where the monument may be sited in the center of a city; *the three women* in whose minds the unknown prisoner is remembered and who set the whole dramatic context of the monument; and the *tower* intended as an easily identified symbol which both suggests the tyranny of persecution and the capacity of man to rise beyond it."[11]

Once it has the life-size scale planned for it, the spectator will be able to

Left: Butler: *The Unknown Political Prisoner* (project for a monument). (1951-53). Bronze with stone base, 17⅞" high. The Museum of Modern Art, New York, Saidie A. May Fund

Right: Butler: *Figure in Space*. (1957-58). Bronze, 35¼" high. Pierre Matisse Gallery, New York

42

Butler: *Girl.* (1954-56). Bronze, 7′ 5″ high.
Pierre Matisse Gallery, New York

identify more readily with the three women and their upward gaze, while their self-contained silhouette should also set up the necessary esthetic distance. The contrast between the personages in their helpless isolation and the metal tripod create the ambiance of humanity versus the rigid machinery of the state. It is now planned to erect the monument on a height in West Berlin, and it seems fitting that it should stand in Germany.

The open structure of *The Unknown Political Prisoner* took on a specific referential function, as did the figures below it. Butler's development since that time has definitely been in the direction of greater naturalism. At first glance his evolution from rather abstract, open, welded sculpture to his recent, more naturalistic, closed, modeled bronzes seems to reverse the history of sculpture in the twentieth century. But it must be remembered that Butler's change took place after the mid-century, at a time when earlier innovations—including his own—had already frozen into clichés and much of the welding of iron rods had become tinkering rather than formal experiment.

The *Girl* of 1954-56 (page 43) has the intense vitality of erotic recognition. This heroic bronze figure, erect, taut, stretching upward from the thin grid on which she stands, reaches yearningly toward the object of her desire. Each of the round, conal, and columnar forms re-emphasizes the basic conception of unsatisfied sensuality. The very recent *Figure in Space* (page 42) is a full female torso, swinging on an iron spit. In the spear-like form of this grid-armature supporting a heavy, curved, voluptuous female body, Butler set himself a problem in formal relationship of solid mass twisting in open space; it is a provocative synthesis of his early thin, welded, insectile figures and the later hedonistic nudes.

COSMO CAMPOLI born 1922

Imaginative forces, creative forces, penetrative forces, fall through the funnel which is the artist, and through his hands; like a caterpillar turning into a moth, the transformed image is evolved.

Cosmo Campoli, Chicago, April 1959

When the iconography of the mid-twentieth century is studied, it seems likely that birth and death will be encountered as two of the leading themes of contemporary artists. With the vanishing belief in any pre-established dogma and the lack of collective myth in our culture, artists have turned to the two certainties of man's existence.

Birth and death are the principal subjects which have occupied Campoli's attention as a sculptor, but his sculptural forms differ markedly from the prevailing style of their time. While most sculpture is open, linear and transparent, Campoli's is closed, massive and block-like. He has never chosen to weld, but carves and prefers to model in clay. He speaks of a need to have his "hand rooted in clay which gives sustenance to the sculptor's being and is the anchor that holds him to the earth from which all life springs," and his surfaces, for instance, tend to retain a pitted, earthy quality.

Typical of this aspect of his work is *Birth of Death* of 1950 (page 46). Quite possibly influenced in its inception by the squat Aztec goddess of childbirth, this bronze is a considerably more complex construction. Not only frontal, but bisymmetrical, it has a secondary axis across the torso from which the legs and arms come out with concentrated gesture. Like paws the fists cover the eyes, where shadows create enormous cavities, while the convex forehead repeats the swelling of the belly.

Birth of 1958 (page 47) deals with the same theme. The problem of the base has here been fully resolved with the child itself supporting its birth-giving mother. The whole concept is abstracted further, moving beyond personality: it is a concrete yet universalized image of the *act* of giving birth, the forms suggesting the violent, thrusting rhythm of the female body in the last stages of labor. "My sculpture," Campoli says, "is not made to match walls, to please or not to please anyone, or to make some damn dog happy, but to have its own personality and exist as a strong personality exists. My sculpture is, and shall

Campoli: *Birth of Death*. (1950). Bronze, 33″ high. Allan
Frumkin Gallery, Chicago

Campoli: *Birth.* (1958). Plaster model for bronze, 39" high. Allan Frumkin Gallery, Chicago

Campoli: *Mother and Child.* (1958). Marble, 7″ high. Allan Frumkin Gallery, Chicago

be, strong enough to make an ash tray alongside of it look only like an ash tray."[12]

A large mass, apparently yielding a smaller substance below it—the form of *Birth of Death* and *Birth*—appears again in the *Return of the Prodigal Son* of 1959 (opposite), where the minor figure of the son kneels below a large, indeed an enormous, head made up of a multitude of faces. These faces with their bulbous noses and bulging eyes are beneficent and terrible, threatening and gratified. The great head floats, disembodied, above a throne, covering the top of it like a cloud. It is the Godhead, both male and female, angry and kind, and burgeoning like the flames of the burning bush.

Like ancient sculptures made to propitiate hostile spirits, Campoli's work also has the quality—found among many of the artists presented here—of conjuring up supernatural aid. That is to say, for the artist, the work partakes somewhat of the character of a fetish or shaman: it is, among other things, a magical image to control the irrational world.

48

Campoli: *Return of the Prodigal Son.* (1957-59). Plaster model for bronze, 30″ high. Allan Frumkin
Gallery, Chicago

CÉSAR   born 1921

César Baldacchini does not work in a sculptor's studio; he has instead a small workshop in a factory in the suburbs of Paris. There, in Saint-Denis, he assembles old scraps of iron and pieces of machinery and welds them into sculptures. In *Torso* (opposite), for example, he has built a fretwork of heavy iron wire in the back of the figure which supports the shell of the body itself. This torso consists of a great number of small, irregular iron plates as well as tubes, pipes and nails which are fused into a more or less continuous surface. In certain areas, such as the breasts and the inner thighs, these smooth plates are clearly visible, while elsewhere they have been worked in and melted down below a corruscated surface. The result is that the body appears to have been eaten away rather than shattered. Starting with "ready-made" materials of industry and using the methods of modern technology, César has come forth conversely with a sinister nude whose decay resembles that of time—a savage assertion of the corruption and frailty of the once undefiled flesh.

César's earlier subjects included chickens, fishes, insects and all manner of fabled beasts; frequently a piece would change its identity during the working process. Today he seems preoccupied with his version of the human figure for which, however, he seems to have sacrificed none of his supernatural fantasy.

The skin of his nudes (pages 52, 54) evokes association with the scales of fishes and skins of reptiles, and he sometimes seems to be consciously alluding to primeval and legendary creatures who are in the state of evolution along an imaginary philogenetic tree. The winged figures, such as the one on page 53, refer to man during a strange metamorphosis. His single enormous wing, growing violently out of the torso deprives him of both head and arms. It is like a thwarted stage of evolution toward Homo sapiens. Or does this figure merely allude to the ancient fable of Icarus; to man's great dream of being winged and the inevitable result of his attempt at flight?

César: *Torso.* (1954). Welded iron, 30½" high. Private collection, New York

César: *Nude of Saint-Denis, I.* (1956). Forged and welded iron, 36″ high. Collection Robert Elkon, New York

Winged Figure. (c. 1957). Cast iron, 56″ long. Collection Mr. and Mrs. Richard K. Weil, St. Louis

César: *Nude of Saint-Denis, IV.* (1957). Bronze, 24¼″ high.
The Hanover Gallery, London

RICHARD DIEBENKORN   born 1922

Painting in the San Francisco Bay Area before and during the War consisted largely of landscapes, seascapes and cityscapes in which precise lines were superimposed on thinly painted color patches. There was also a belated influence coming from Mexican mural painting. In the mid-Forties, however, the California School of Fine Arts under the direction of Douglas McAgy established a meeting ground for advanced painters, which served as a stimulus against the prevailing styles of watered-down Dufy and palatable Rivera. Clyfford Still taught there from 1946 until 1950, and Mark Rothko during the summers of 1947 and 1949. These men did not exert any direct stylistic influence, but their uncompromising individuality, their high regard for the position of the artist, their vigorous working processes and their penetration into unexplored territory had a liberating effect of great importance.

Richard Diebenkorn, born in Portland, Oregon, had been a student at Stanford University and the University of California before going to the California School of Fine Arts for a year of study in 1946. He then taught at this school from 1947 to 1950. The paintings which first brought him recognition were large canvases in which light colors expanded in flowing forms upon a basic horizontal-vertical structure. Non-objective in character, they yet had associations with vistas of land or sea in which the open vastness of Western space found its pictorial equivalent.

In 1955 Diebenkorn followed the older David Park and Elmer Bischoff by departing from his own version of action painting and turning to a figurative style which combines the idiom of abstract expressionism with the surrealist, the expressionist, and the fauve heritage.[13] Since that time he has mainly concentrated on pictures with one or two personages in an interior or against a landscape vista. His palette—ultramarines, apple greens, cadmiums, siennas, umbers—has become more sensuous, clearly recalling the canvases of Matisse. Diebenkorn's color, however, is brushed on more roughly and spontaneously, with splashes of paint left visible in the finished picture.

The asymmetric structure of verticals and horizontals is now of even greater importance than in his earlier work in its relationship to the squarish format of his canvases. The figure is the specific area of concentration, the gathering point of emphasis in the picture. It is here that the directional lines converge, that color becomes most intense and the pattern more varied. Thus the spaciousness of the surrounding areas is greatly enhanced by the familiar measure of the

Diebenkorn: *Girl on a Terrace*. (1956). Oil on canvas, 71 × 66". Collection Mr. and Mrs. Roy R. Neuberger, New York

orn: *Girl with Cups.* 1957.
canvas, 59 × 54". Collection
Brown Baker, New York

human figure. The faces, generally, are barely indicated, but his large personages, awkward and isolated in an ambiguous but always empty space of muted
interiors or brillant landscapes, testify to their insular presence. Diebenkorn
is interested above all in conveying his feelings about color and space. The
figure is used as the empathetic protagonist of this color-space relationship.

Diebenkorn: *Man and Woman in a Large Room.* 1957. Oil on canvas, 71 × 63″. Collection Joseph H. Hirshhorn, New York

iebenkorn: *Man and Woman Seated*. (1958). Oil on canvas, 70½ × 83½". Collection Mr. and Mrs. William Zeckendorf, Jr., New York

JEAN DUBUFFET   born 1901

I have attempted to carry the human image (as well as all other subjects dealt with in my paintings) immediately into the range of effectiveness without passing through esthetics. Esthetics bores me, doesn't interest me at all. The slightest intervention of esthetics obstructs for me the efficiency of functioning and spoils the sauce. That is why I try to reject from my works all that could have the smell of esthetics. People with a short-sighted view have concluded from this that I enjoy painting ugly objects. Not at all! I don't worry about their being ugly or beautiful; furthermore these terms are meaningless for me; I even have the conviction that they are meaningless for everybody; I don't believe that these notions of ugliness or beauty have the slightest foundation: they are illusions. I have liked to carry the human image onto a plane of seriousness where the futile embellishments of esthetics have no longer any place, onto a plane of high ceremony, of solemn office of celebration, by helping myself with what Joseph Conrad calls: "a mixture of familiarity and terror," out of which the devotion is made which many religious minds offer to their gods and which does not, at times, exclude the use of swear words directed at them. Where the connivance is total, where the attachment and esteem is unchangeable, there a new language governs: rugged, elliptical and unconstrained. I hope one will understand from these brief indications, how far the mood in which I have painted these personages is removed from that of buffoonery which one has so generously attributed to me. My position is exclusively that of celebration, and whoever has thought to detect in it intentions of humor or satire, of bitterness or invective, has misunderstood it.

Jean Dubuffet, Paris, February 1959

Jean Dubuffet is perhaps the most significant French painter who has emerged since the war. He was born in Le Havre in 1901 and for a short time studied painting at the Académie Julian, but then went into his family's wine business, a career which he interrupted a good many times in an attempt to escape from a humdrum bourgeois existence. In the mid-Thirties he made masks and marionettes and worked as a puppeteer. He and his friends used plaster, papier-maché, pastes and many odd substances to make masks of their own faces, giving Dubuffet a new feeling for materials and their textures, as well as new imagery. The close relationship between man and his mask—the real and the grotesque—has been retained throughout Dubuffet's work.

He made frequent attempts at painting but returned to it seriously only in

Dubuffet: *Childbirth*. 1944. Oil on canvas, 39⅞ × 31¼". Collection Mr. and Mrs. Pierre Matisse, New York

1942. His first exhibition, held immediately after the Liberation in October 1944, antagonized the public to such an extent that some of his paintings were destroyed despite the presence of armed guards. In the most shocking terms he had expressed the flimsiness of our existence, had even questioned the existence itself.

Making masks, collecting the "art" of the insane and untutored, studying cult images, Dubuffet had been searching not only for the sources of creative inspiration, but for visible signs to express the very sources of life. *Childbirth* of 1944 (page 61), dates back to his first exhibition. The bright flat colors, the very child-like execution with its naive frontal vision, the simplified drawing, come much closer to children's art than does the work of more sophisticated painters like Klee and Miró who have also been inspired by the same source. *Childbirth* captures the naïveté of votive pictures; it is like those thank offerings found in pilgrimage churches and presents a comparable aspect of ritual, of "emotion recollected in tranquillity," which is as applicable to a religious celebration as to a work of art. In the statement Dubuffet wrote for this book, he speaks of ceremony and celebration, and indeed these are key concepts for the comprehension of his work, because Dubuffet celebrates the human comedy in all its tragic aspects.

Dubuffet has always been fascinated by the *graffiti*—rude scratchings found on walls all the way from paleolithic caves to those of the modern metropolis. The *Archetypes* (opposite) was the first of a series of *graffiti* made by the artist in 1945. The bold outlines of the coarse figures are incised into a dark and heavy ground. They remind us of the ancient convention of Egyptian painting with the frontal torso and the profile head, but they reject all the refinements of Egyptian painting in favor of a more primitive treatment. The material, a paste resembling an alchemist's concoction, is made out of innumerable ingredients besides sand, earth and water, to which the pigment is added. Dubuffet's color and light are really functions of the pigment, which is of extreme importance to him as it is to many of the artists of his generation. Yet he controls his material in order to permit the discordant image to emerge. He may throw on his paint like an angry child, quickly drawing a picture of Teacher, but his grotesque man with yellow teeth and grasshopper limbs (page 64) differs from the child's drawing in the intensity of the confrontation. Notwithstanding its cruel savagery this is a sympathetic, almost humorous "portrait." This fellow is more basic than Organization Man. Presented front-on and directly, violent and violated, distorted and agonized, the wild clown is still gesturing agressively, urging not pity but compassion.

Between April 1950 and February 1951 Dubuffet, whose output is phenomenal, painted about fifty pictures of the female nude. These *Corps de Dames* (page 65) are coarsely textured maps of the female body. The Western tradition of beauty and grace, indeed all of man's illusion about woman are destroyed by a savage evocation of a never-eradicated archetype going back to paleolithic stone effigies of fertility.

Dubuffet is related to surrealism, not in style but in basic attitude. He feels very strongly "that the key to things must not be as we imagine it, but that the world must be ruled by strange systems of which we have not the slightest

Dubuffet: *Dhotel with Yellow Teeth.* (1947)
Mixed media on canvas, 45¼ × 35".
Private collection, New York

inkling."[14] He searches after ambiguity to come closer to the revelation of the true nature of things. His *Woman with Furs* (page 66) is a conglomeration of lichens or organisms seen under a microscope. It recalls the sixteenth-century figures of Arcimboldo constructed out of fruits and vegetables: an image made up of items which are quite unrelated to the image itself; a metaphor on metamorphosis.

Similarly *The Dunce Cap* (page 67) has the appearance of chameleonlike change. In the mid-Fifties Dubuffet invented his own form of collage—the *assemblage*—in which paintings cut into pieces are re-assembled on a new surface and permitted, often quite accidentally to take on new shapes and meanings.

Dubuffet: *"Corps de dame — l'oursonne."* (1950).
Oil on canvas, 45¾ × 35".
Pierre Matisse Gallery, New York

Playing with these pieces, he will catch an image before it glides away, paste it down, and paint around its outlines, permitting the patchwork surface to preserve aspects of equivocation.

Like Schwitters, Dubuffet has collected the debris of civilization. He has made sculpture out of sponges, slag and lava, charred wood, steel wool, broken glass. The *Knight of Darkness* (page 66) is an aggregation of slag and clinkers. This phantom, ominously confronting us, could be both an oracle of our nuclear future and a furnace gnome, product of an artist's eye which seeks its release for fantasy in any casual cast-off object. This equivocal aspect—the "mixture of familiarity and terror"—is the major motif of Dubuffet's work.

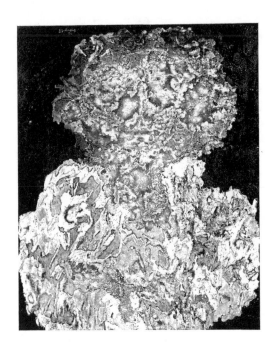 

Left: Dubuffet: *Woman with Furs.* 1954. Oil on canvas, 39½ x 32″. Collection Mr. and Mrs. Ralph F. Colin, New York

Right: Dubuffet: *Knight of Darkness.* (1954). Slag and clinkers, 35½″ high. Collection Mr. and Mrs. Albert A. List, New York

66

Dubuffet: *The Dunce Cap ("La pointe au pitre")*. 1956. Assemblage on canvas, 57 × 45¼". Pierre Matisse Gallery. New York

ALBERTO GIACOMETTI   born 1901

You ask me about my artistic intentions concerning the human image. I do not know how to answer your question very well.

Sculpture, painting and drawing have always been for me the means by which I render to myself an account of my vision of the outer world and particularly of the face and the human being in its entirety or, more simply, of my fellow creatures and, particularly, of those who, for one reason or another, are the closest to me.

Reality for me has never been a pretext to make art objects, but art a necessary means to render to myself a better account of what I see. Hence the position I take with regard to my conception of art is a completely traditional one.

Yet, I know that it is utterly impossible for me to model, paint or draw a head, for instance, as I see it and, still, this is the only thing I am attempting to do. All that I will be able to make will be only a pale image of what I see and my success will always be less than my failure or, perhaps, the success will be equal to my failure. I do not know whether I work in order to make something or in order to know why I cannot make what I would like to make.

It may be that all this is nothing but an obsession, the causes of which I do not know, or a compensation for a deficiency somewhere. In any case, I recognize now that your question is much too vast or too general for me to answer in a precise manner. By asking this simple question you have, in fact, put everything in question, so how answer it?

Alberto Giacometti, Paris, May 17, 1959

Giacometti was born in the same year as Dubuffet, but has been fully engaged in sculpture and painting since 1914. The son of an impressionist landscape painter, he was born in Stampa, Switzerland, and studied at the Ecole des Arts et Métiers in Geneva. During an early trip to Italy he admired Tintoretto, Giotto and Cimabue above all others. In 1922 he arrived in Paris and studied at the Académie de la Grande Chaumière under Antoine Bourdelle. He writes of those days in the Twenties when he felt it impossible to grasp a whole head and when figures were never closed masses for him but always transparent constructions.

In works such as the *Slaughtered Woman* (1932) and *The Palace at 4 A.M.*

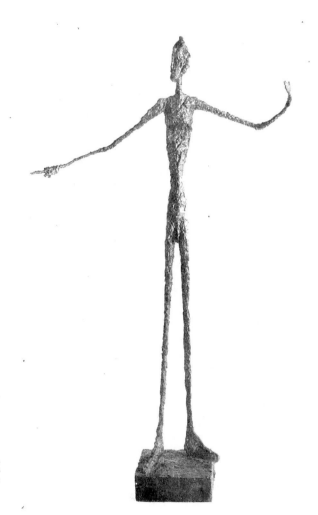

(page 14) he was strongly affected by the surrealist mystique and indeed was an official member of the surrealist group. The "Palace" came to him almost automatically, took form in his mind, and, according to his statements, "attained such reality that its execution in space did not take me more than one day."[15] Eventually, however, he felt that he needed to know more about the human figure. He thought this study would take about two weeks, but "I worked with the model all day from 1935 to 1940."[16] Then he began shaping his figures from memory, but his sculpture became too small and the figures achieved a resemblance only when long and bone-thin. "It was necessary to go to the very end, and see what can be done,"[17] and Giacometti, working in that pliant material, plaster, built and destroyed, had visions and tried to capture them before they eluded his fantasy.

The range of subjects over the last twelve years is very limited: mostly tall, standing figures for which his brother Diego or his wife Annette were the models (page 69, 72). There is an occasional head of Diego (page 75), a seated version of Annette, or he will group his figures to give them paradoxically an even greater feeling of isolation and solitude (opposite).

Dubuffet's figures are seen at exceedingly close range; he analyses a woman's body as if he were looking through a microscope. But Giacometti's figures are very distant. No matter how close we come they remain far away, from each other and from us. Their features do not loom larger as we approach them. Sartre has pointed out in his essay on Giacometti that for centuries sculptors have rendered a model as if she were right in front of them; they described what they knew to be there, not what they actually saw at their distance. Giacometti, however, not wishing to violate man's privacy, maintains his own distance. The existentialist philosopher and writer no longer tries to investigate essences, believing it to be a vain attempt. Camus, characteristically, limits himself to a forthright description of man's thought and action, as it appears to him. Giacometti's remote figures seem to have the same function.

Giacometti is supremely conscious of space, which infringes on everything. Of him, his friend Sartre wrote, "to sculpt for him, is to take the fat off space,"[18] and Richard Wilbur in his poem *Giacometti:* "...no nakedness so bare as flesh gone in inquiring of the bone."[19]. His emaciated figures, although they first appeared at the end of the second World War are not starved survivors of the concentration camps: they are simply human beings—alone, inaccessible, and therefore inviolate.

In the *Man Pointing* of 1947 (page 69), there was still a great emphasis on the gesture—the outstretched arm commanding surrounding space. Later even

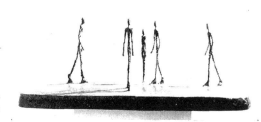

Giacometti: *City Square*. (1949). Bronze, 9¾"
high × 25⅜" long. Collection Mr. and Mrs.
Pierre Matisse, New York

Giacometti: *Composition with Three Figures and a
Head (The Sand)*. (1950). Painted bronze, 22"
high. Collection Philip Johnson, New Canaan,
Connecticut

this disappeared, leaving the isolated figure or simply a hand or a leg alone like an ancient fragment.

It is the ingenious invention of Sartre in *No Exit* to prevent his characters from ever closing their eyes, thus depriving them throughout eternity of man's most blessed release: sleep and loss of consciousness of self and surroundings. Similarly, Giacometti's Tall Figures—erect, distant and immutable—can stand or pace but never rest. Wilbur deals with the force of this tension:

  ....

   And look where Giacometti in a room
   Dim as a cave of the sea, has built the man
   We are, and made him walk:
   Towering like a thin
   Coral, out of a reef of plaster chalk,
   This is the single form we can assume.

  ....

   He is pruned of every gesture, saving only
   The habit of coming and going. Every pace
   shuffles a million feet.
   The faces in this face
   All all forgotten faces of the street
   Gathered to one anonymous and lonely.

   No prince and no Leviathan, he is made
   Of infinite farewells...[20]

ght: Giacometti: *Man Pointing* (see page 69); *Tall Figure.* (1947). Bronze, 6' 7" high. Private collection, New York; *ure.* (1949). Painted bronze, 65" high. Collection Mr. and Mrs. James Thrall Soby, New Canaan, Connecticut

Giacometti: *Man Seated*. 1950. Oil on canvas, 31½ × 25½". Collection Mr. and Mrs. Richard Deutsch, Greenwich, Connecticut

Giacometti: *The Artist's Mother*. 1950. Oil on canvas, 34⅜ × 23½". The Museum of Modern Art, New York, acquired through the Lillie P. Bliss Bequest

GIACOMETTI BY RENÉ CHAR

Some linen spread out, underlinen and house linen, held by pins, was hanging from a line. Its carefree owner had willingly let it stay out all night. A fine white dew was spread over the stones and the grass. Despite the promise of heat, the countryside had not yet ventured to chatter. The beauty of the morning amidst the deserted gardens was complete, for the peasants had not yet opened their door with the great lock and the large key to wake up pails and tools. The poultry yard was claiming its rights. A couple by Giacometti, abandoning the nearby path, appeared on the grounds. Nude or not. Slender and transparent like the windows of burnt-out churches, graceful like ruins which have suffered

74

Giacometti: *Head of Diego*. (1954). Bronze, 26½" high. Collection Mr. and Mrs. Sidney F. Brody, Los Angeles.

much in losing their weight and their ancient blood. Yet proud in bearing in the manner of those who engage themselves without trembling under the relentless light of undergrowth and of disasters. These impassioned lovers of oleander paused in front of the farmer's bush and took in its fragrance for a long time. The wash on the line became frightened. A stupid dog fled without barking. The man touched the belly of the woman who thanked him with a look, tenderly. But only the water in the deep well, under its little roof of granite, rejoiced in this gesture because it understood in it a distant meaning. Inside the house in the rustic bedroom of his friends, the great Giacometti was sleeping.[21]

LEON GOLUB born 1922

My recent paintings can be viewed in various ways:

1 *Man is seen as having undergone a holocaust or facing annihilation or mutation. The ambiguities of these huge forms indicate the stress of their vulnerability versus their capacities for endurance.*

2 *Man is seen in an heroic gesture of the very beauty and sensuous organic vitality of even fragmented forms. The enlarged carnal beauty of the fragment is contrasted to its pathos and monumentality.*

3 *These paintings attempt to reinstate a contemporary catharsis, that measure of man which is related to an existential knowledge of the human condition—a recognition that looks back to the symbolic incarnation of classic art.*

4 *The figures are implacable in their appearance and resistance, stance or stare. They are implacable in the compacted wearing down of surfaces and forms to simpler forms but with more complicated surfaces. They are implacable as they take on the resistance of stone as against the undulations of flesh. They are implacable as they know an absolute state of mind (on the edge of nothingness) just as they know a nearly absolute state of massiveness.*

Leon Golub, Bloomington, Indiana, March 1959

Golub's *Damaged Man* of 1955 (opposite) depicts a tortured yet still human head on a body which has been flattened out into a skin, like the flayed hide of Marsyas. The surface is eroded and encrusted with eruptions as if the life sap had come to the surface of this mutant, whose carcass is all that remains. Yet the *Damaged Man* retains the significance of individual destiny: a pathetic persistence in continuing to exist, in spite of mutilation, symbolizes his endurance and strength.

The apparent contradiction between man's impotence achieved through mutilation and his courage to survive is the key to Golub's imagery. His earlier painting, done in Chicago between 1950 and 1956—the series of burnt men and thwarted men, of kings, priests and ritualistic sphinxes—leaned heavily on

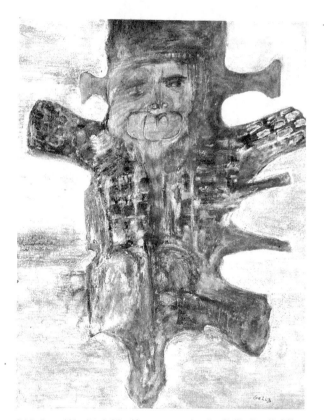

Golub: *Damaged Man*. (1955). Oil and lacquer on masonite, 48 × 36″. Allan Frumkin Gallery, Chicago

Golub: *Colossal Head.* (1958).
lacquer on canvas, 82½ × 48
Frumkin Gallery, Chicago

primitivistic imagery to express his feelings of loneliness and dread. His work then seemed related to the art of the Hittites, the Assyrians, and the Aztecs. A year's visit to Italy in 1956-57, however, not only altered his form, but seemed to increase his faith in human endurance.

He now prefers to emphasize the power of the rational rather than the magical in controlling the irrational and has turned to classical art for his prototype. He admires the heroic gesture and finds measure in the severe constraints of Greek and Roman sculpture. Lacking both arms and neck, *Orestes* (page 81) is a new version of the *Damaged Man*. Called *Orestes*, because he is a symbol of a frustrated youth unable to control his environment, he is a lonely, tragic figure. This canvas was first exhibited at the Institute of Contemporary Art in London in 1957. Lawrence Alloway remarked on its relationship to ancient marbles: "Common to Golub's massive single figures is the idea of sculptural status as a symbol of the human condition. In *Orestes* the state of a sculpture is taken as a literal representation of an anguished and vulnerable human being. The body is the container of a shocked, surprised consciousness."[22]

The *Horseman* (page 80) and the *Colossal Head* (opposite), both painted in 1958, become more classical in restraint, less mutilated in body. Golub paints strong, virile figures of authority with the introspective stare, the "inward look" which is found in the Constantine giants of fourth-century Rome. This was the time when the Empire was no longer able to stave off chaos and disaster, when, with the vanishing of the values of the classical world, man became increasingly introspective and full of anxiety and turned to the mystery cults of the East. Golub's colossal figures face the destiny of their isolation with implacability.

Size is important in these paintings and the artist had to choose a scale larger than that of his own measure to emphasize the monumentality and power of his figures and to enhance their psychological impact. The *Reclining Youth* (page 82) is huge without, however, assuming the distortions of a giant. The position of this figure is based on the *Dying Gaul* from Pergamon,[23] but instead of its baroque recessions, the *Reclining Youth* is thrust into the frontal plane, brutalized and reduced to more simple and primitive articulation.

If the body seems mutilated and the skin gnawed at, the canvas itself has become a celebration in paint. Golub applies successive coats of lacquers, carves into the surface with a sculpture tool, removes the pigment with solvents, rebuilds and recoats until he achieves his texture, which in its opulent and sensuous quality is a sign of deep affirmation of the magnificence of man and, indeed, of the classic tradition.

Golub: *Horseman.* (1958). Oil and lacquer o1
84 × 96". Collection Mrs. Herbert S. Gr
Chicago

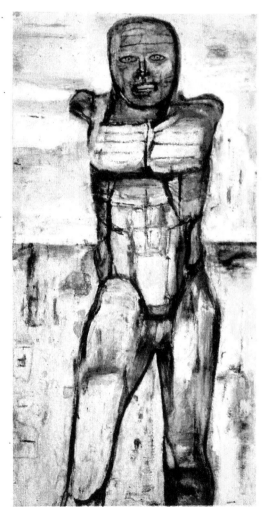

ıb: *Orestes*. (1956). Oil and lacquer on canvas,
42″. Collection Mr. and Mrs. Lewis Manilow,
ago

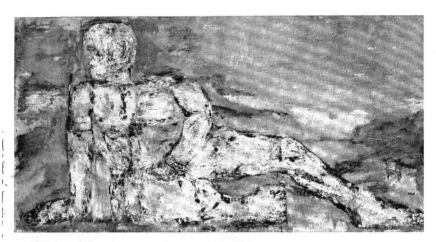

Golub: *Reclining Youth*. (1959). Oil and lacquer on canvas, 6′ 7″ × 13′ 9″. Collection Mr. and Mrs. Lewis Manilow, Chicago

BALCOMB GREENE   born 1904

Before 1942 I considered my work completely non-representational and was active in developing a theoretical basis for this practice. I was the first chairman of American Abstract Artists in 1937, and kept this position two more years. Since 1942 I have worked back to an apparent imagery or representation. The best I can say for a motive is that I "felt in my bones" that I had to go that way. Any theoretical position which I now take rests upon this feeling, and upon its gathering force.

Painting devoid of conscious imagery can be powerful, but it seems to me this power has lessened after Mondrian. The language of abstraction, like an earlier language of visual accuracy, was most powerful while being learned.

Man is difficult to present in painting because it was done so badly by the end of the last century, but also because he seems to our disillusioned minds not worth presenting. I see no point in using him for compositional purposes, because his proportions are naturally pleasing to himself, or in order to repeat the dreary truth of his corruption, his weakness and his self-preoccupation. We should have a respite from the ugly and agonized faces which are turned to us by people without dignity, who demand pity. We should understand that the Christian compassion which is the principal note in the early Rouaults, must have a miserable evolution. Essential to it is a repudiation of the flesh. Its inevitable sequel is the Pierrot or sad clown of Rouault, no longer presenting the generalized love, but man alone without sex and without energy—in love with himself. The safest treatment of compassion in art should emphasize him who, without self-destruction, must feel it. Whoever represents man, assumes a moral risk. Great art must give him more energy, and more virtue of a kind or more heroism, than we commonly find in him.

The method is worn out whereby the artist follows his private style and permits the brush strokes to arrange themselves to suggest a figure, with an accidental grotesqueness which pretends seriousness. When the brush misbehaves or the paint drips, such a seriousness is inevitable. A return to consciousness in the studio, to an adult and even intellectual consciousness, is the next move. The doctrine of a pure esthetic which disdains the image of man, can only be disputed from the moralist's position, by those who wish to live. It is in his violations of such a compact doctrine, but especially in his lapses from the common, the social and the useful virtues, that the artist renews himself.

It is dangerous to seek in words for the extraordinary and neglected virtues. Somehow they have to do with an overflowing sexuality, courage which grows with it, and an awareness of death. These are not utilities, are not the common virtues, but are goodness in themselves. No need to be more definite than this.

Greene: *Seated Woman.* (1954). Oil on canvas, 48 × 38″. Bertha Schaefer
Gallery, New York

Greene: *Gertrude, II.* 1956-58. Oil on canvas, 64 × 49⅜″. Collec
and Mrs. Joseph Weinstein, New York

No need to crusade against the pure non-objectivists, who may continue their accomplishments. They may even dance with a certain dignity, as Schopenhauer would describe it, on the edge of the abyss. If worst comes to worst we can join them. We can close our eyes. The thing to dread is mankind's small vision, his shrinking vision, of himself.

Balcomb Greene, Montauk Point, May 1959

Greene was born in 1904 in Niagara Falls, New York. He studied literature, philosophy, the history of art and psychology in New York and in Vienna. He taught English literature at Dartmouth College, and since 1952 he has been professor of the history of art and esthetics at the Carnegie Institute of Technology in Pittsburgh. He is, however, primarily a painter, although in painting he has had no formal training. In the Thirties Greene worked in a geometric-abstract style and in 1937 and 1939 he presided as chairman of the American Abstract Artists, that highly important, though somewhat restrictive group which kept abstract art alive in America during a time when it was considered esoteric and branded as un-American.

Greene's murals at the New York World's Fair of 1939 were still geometrically constructed, hard-edged and flatly painted, but soon thereafter his work began to grow looser and to open up like that of many artists at that time. Since then, for almost twenty years now, he has been engaged in an attempt to capture a vague image, to lead it into the realm of the sensuous and even the heroic without ever returning to former modes of expression.

Greene spends most of his time by the sea near Montauk Point, Long Island; light and air have permeated his paintings, indeed, determine his forms, so that his once solid shapes have been shattered by light. Although he works from elaborate sketches, his canvases remain records of the painter's spontaneous movement. Often it is difficult to recognize the subject in his paintings because light remains the primary element in his work. At times, as in *Gertrude, II* (page 85), a whole series of multiple images leaps into our vision only to recede into the active tissue of the painting itself. The distinction between figure and ground is left ambiguous: instead the whole canvas participates in a dynamic movement which is communicated to the viewer. It is the total experience of seeing the interaction of light, color, woman, space.

Greene: *Anguish*. (1956). Oil on canvas, 48 × 60". Bertha Schaefer Gallery, New York

de Kooning: *Woman.* (1950). Oil on canvas, 64 × 46″. Department of Art, The Woman's College of the University of North Carolina, Greensboro

WILLEM DE KOONING   born 1904

In 1916 when de Kooning was twelve years old he started working as an apprentice in a decorator's shop in his native Rotterdam and soon after that he began to study at the Academie voor Beeldende Kunsten in the evenings. There, he says, young art students ran the gamut from rigid academicians who made them copy plaster casts to young instructors who, as members of the avant garde, exposed them to the geometric abstraction of de Stijl. While de Kooning was very much attracted to Mondrian, his taste was broad enough to include van Gogh and the prevailing background of Art Nouveau's evocative convoluting line. After graduating in 1924, he continued studying painting and design in Brussels and Antwerp and then came to the United States in 1926. He was at first a house painter in New Jersey, then a commercial artist in New York. Like most of his contemporaries, in the mid-Thirties, he worked on the WPA Federal Art Project. It was then that his painting became more abstract. In 1939 he did murals for the New York World's Fair but when asked about them now, he does not seem to remember them too fondly. It took a relatively long time for de Kooning to develop into a mature and significant painter, and nourishment from a great many sources was necessary. He himself talks about Picasso, Giacometti, Miró, Stuart Davis and his very close friend Arshile Gorky.

In the early Forties he had done pictures of women which were still largely cubist in their form; he then exploded these restrictions upon vehement large surfaces. His black-and-white and his cream-colored paintings of irregular shapes and calligraphic interlacings—restless rhythms expanding in a compact space—were among the most original commitments made by an artist to the creative process itself. De Kooning was known and admired for this work by his fellow-artists a long time before his first one-man show at the Egan Gallery in 1948. By this time he was already in the center of attention in the new movement in American painting.

Then in 1949 the figure came back into his work, and everyone was surprised and nobody seemed to know why. Recently I asked de Kooning whether it was really true, as has often been suggested, that the working process itself, the actual act of painting, evoked these women on the canvas. He did not think so. He said he was definitely interested in painting Woman, a figure, just as throughout the ages artists have made symbols of female goddesses or cult images. It was a traditional idea, and he felt that he wanted to continue the Western tradition by painting the symmetrical female figure, but he also

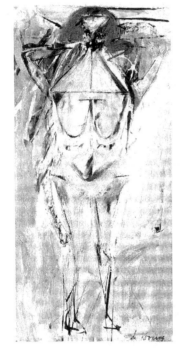

de Kooning: *Figure in Landscape, No. 2.* (1951).
Oil on canvas, 33½ × 16½". Collection Joseph
H. Hirshhorn, New York

de Kooning: *Woman, I.* (1950-52). Oil on canvas,
The Museum of Modern Art, New York. Purchas

wanted to make a new figure and "it had to be stark."

He would receive a rapid image when a woman walked into a room; it was essential to catch that glimpse, and he tied the image down quickly; knowing where the head and legs had to be placed, and not leaving very much space between them. Then he would cut mouths out of magazines—the toothy smiles of Miss Rheingold—and pasted them on his paintings. But he didn't want to make collages; these, after all, had been done, so he painted in his own mouths with their mocking grins and the picture became frantic.

"Are they horrible, masochistic women whose distortion expresses great suffering?" De Kooning feels that they are also humorous. After all, there is the atom bomb, a world in turmoil; it would drive one insane to face all the implications. Therefore relief, tragi-comic relief, is needed, and the Women combine comedy with tragedy. He sees humor in them—the angry humor of tragedy.

He painted these shamelessly erotic women close-up, in immediate encounter, giving us the feeling of uncanny familiarity and presence and simultaneously destroying classic proportions. Their large, square frames, he feels, are male as well as female; but above all female. He did not work from models, because to him the model would be a real woman and not a posed set-up. But he looked at photographs in the men's magazines, cut them out, and turned them upside down, constantly changing parts to get new and surprising realities. Thighs became arms and vice versa, giving the figure a new and powerful twist. The breasts had to be large, not so much, he says, for the psychological reasons which some interpreters have suggested, but because the vigorous movement of his arm naturally made large, sweeping curves.

After the black-and-white canvases, color came back when he painted the women. Why, he asks, if Gauguin made figures yellow and Picasso painted them blue, couldn't one use flesh color? After all, Rubens did masterfully, and "Flesh was the reason why oil painting was invented"[24] in the first place. So he painted the women in almost vulgar flesh colors, and then other colors appeared: violets, vermilions, oranges, lemon yellows and biting greens.

It was important to paint the Women, de Kooning recalls. Yet his paintings remained abstract. It is as if the abstract forms were invested with more specific symbols of anger, pain, humor. But the pictorial needs of the painting itself continued to determine the forms and colors. And now, after an interval of some years devoted almost entirely to non-figurative painting, he says that he expects to paint the figure once more—men as well as women—exploring new possibilities which will derive from his most recent achievement.

Kooning: *Woman and Bicycle*.
152-53). Oil on canvas, 76½ × 49".
1itney Museum of American Art,
w York

de Kooning: *Two Women's Torsos*. (1952). Pastel, 18¾ × 24". The Art Institute of Chicago, the John H. Wrenn Fund

de Kooning: *Marilyn Monroe*. (1954). Oil on canvas, 30 × 30". Collection Mr. and Mrs. Roy R. Neuberger, New York

95

RICO LEBRUN   born 1900

In painting, as in everything else, I prefer situations which make both myself and the image vulnerable, and thus open to risk as well as to discovery. Design is for me the speech of form tried and altered by vicissitudes. And because of this, the human figure is my favorite subject; I prefer its vertical, horizontal and oblique gestures to all other propositions of abstraction, being convinced that they are the richest and most alive in every sense.

Because of my place of birth, I am, essentially, in love with wall painting. By wall painting I mean the tragic arabesque, organic and pertinent as a seismograph, and not the descriptive nor the historical. Paradoxically enough I call what I wish to do Interior decoration. But the "Interior" has here another meaning, and the room, the parlor I wish to speak about, is in the edifice of man.

The painter, faced with the contest between freewheeling ego expression itself, and the canonical points of the figure questioning this expression, has a hard task. In the words of Emily Dickinson, he finds that, if "A Bone has obligations, a Being has the same."

I believe that if an authentic, unprecedented image of man is to appear, it will only be through a complete acceptance of that obligation to sponsor, reveal and celebrate man's condition. This is a subject which cannot be prefabricated by conceits, but may condescend, now and then, to be measured by love. Its terrain is immense. We have so far only written postcards about "wishing to be there," or at best made trial trips, and, in trying to cross it, have often thrown in the sponge, and achieved those silhouettes of capitulation which pass for "style." For sight and mind are dull and frequently unequal to the task of shaping Composition with the same appalling unity man can maintain through the most terrible reverses. He is the organic and spiritual marvel and the text for revelations.

In the painting of Buchenwald and Dachau I wanted to express the belief that the human image, even when disfigured by the executioner, is grand in meaning. No brutality will ever cancel that meaning. Painting may increase it by changing what is disfigured into what is transfigured.

The theme is about those who disappeared and are no longer mentioned. When their hour struck and they were dumped in the pit, the dial of their limbs marked the awful time of day. So composition was born out of the shocked heart. First a man, second a draughts-

Buchenwald Pit. (1955). Charcoal on canvas, 8′ 2″ × 6′ 8¼″. Jacques Seligmann & Co., New York

Lebrun: *"Dable Disparate."* (1958). Casein and oil
on board, 84 × 45½". Owned by the artist

man, I had to find out for myself that pain has a geometry of its own; and that my being, through a revulsion against all tolerable and manageable skill, wanted to speak out in a single shout.

It is this coincidence of ink or paint with the sentiments, which I hope to find now more and more in my work as I proceed. Compassion and the resolute heart shall be the only guides, shall be, in fact, the technique.

Rico Lebrun, New Haven, Conn., 1959

Rico Lebrun was born in Naples in 1900. Intermittently between 1916 and 1921 he attended night classes at the Academia di Belle Arti in Naples, but a more important factor in his formation as a painter was his close association with the large frescoes and the monumental sculpture in the baroque churches of that city. In 1924 he came to the United States and worked as a commercial artist in New York until 1935 when he received his first Guggenheim grant. In 1937 he settled in California, where he became the recognized leader of a number of prominent artists.

His early paintings—his beggars, clowns, cripples and street musicians—some of which were included in the exhibition "Americans 1942" at the Museum of Modern Art, showed the influence of Italian and Spanish baroque painting and were highly romantic in mood. It was only by slow and deliberate stages that he achieved his unique dramatic monumentality. From 1947 to 1950 he was engaged in his most ambitious undertaking—the "Crucifixion Series"[25]—where he had the courage to use a subject most heavily weighted with tradition for a revelant communication of "man's blindness and inhumanity." The broken-up, almost disparate forms and the agitated restless line of some two hundred paintings and drawings, which made up the great cycle, express the fragmented character of modern disaster.

If some of Lebrun's figures for the *Crucifixion* were done under the undeniable impact of Picasso's *Guernica*, his work in the early Fifties went through a re-evaluation of formal means. From a two-year stay in Mexico the artist returned with a series of vast abstract collages which manifested a new approach to form, combining brilliant, flat color with powerful shape. By pasting down large pieces of paper, he worked out a system of two-dimensional space relationships which strengthened his powers of composition.

Commenting on the *Crucifixion* series he had written: "The crying women are, like all bereaved mothers, empty houses pierced by screams, for I have never seen pretty sorrow."[26] Lebrun, whose work was always characterized by moral outrage and human passion, was now ready to approach the theme of the concentration camp and the gas chamber. The concentration camp series—the paintings and drawings of Buchenwald and Dachau—are frighteningly real pictures of death and disintegration. At the same time they use the contemporary device of multiple imagery. Forms are part of a visual rhythm relating to one another as in multiple exposures. The drawing, *Buchenwald Pit* of 1955 (page 96), is still rather static in its symmetrical composition and seems to express a carefully structured architecture of horror. The *Study for Dachau Chamber* (opposite) of 1958 makes use of cinematic frame devices to link the thrusting and pushing baroque elements to a mid-twentieth century conception of time.

These paintings, murals in both concept and scale, are reminiscent of the later Gothic frescoes by Orcagna, and, especially of Francesco Traini's *Triumph of Death* in the Campo Santo in Pisa.[27] In these grotesquely beautiful pictures, there is a similar rigid symmetry combined with the simultaneous representation of events. Moreover, the same moral and philosophical purpose is apparent in the terrifying figures of Death and of demons, the crowd of leprous beggars, and the procession of fatuous nobles passing before the open coffins containing the rotten cadavers of bishops and kings—the Quick and the Dead. Lebrun saw and studied these frescoes in Pisa, and in 1930 he climbed all over the Cathedral of Orvieto and copied Signorelli's *Last Judgement*; he never forgot the Renaissance painter's energetic action and austere agony of the nude, almost skinned, human body, submitted to the eternal physical punishments of hell.

Lebrun, perhaps more than any other artist discussed here, must be seen in the light of Western tradition. In addition to Traini, Signorelli and Picasso, his work bears—in the *Crucifixion* series—a close relationship to Grünewald's Isenheim Altarpiece, but it is perhaps Goya to whom Lebrun now has the closest affinity. In Goya he finds "all that the human cage can contain of malice, lust, contradiction and splendor expressed in the world of paint, a world of maniacs dolled up like butterflies, or the dual image to express what we all carry in us."[28]

The *Doble Disparate* of 1958 (page 98) is a large superhuman figure silhouetted against a background which barely suggests a landscape. Sitting firmly on the columnar support of the leg is a heavy, violently twisting torso surmounted by the double image of a head with wide-open, contorted mouths and holes for eyes. The heads are flattened out, isolated in space. The expression contrasts with the splendor of the vibrant color which now achieves the effect of fluid spontaneity.

Lebrun: *Study for Dachau Chamber*, 1958. Oil on canvas, 6' 6½" × 7'. Jacques Seligmann & Co., New York

JAMES McGARRELL   born 1930

Neither the presence nor the absence of the figure or any other subject guarantees anything about the quality of painting today. I am stuck with the figure because I am too hopelessly anthropomorphic to disembody the gesture in a painting without dehumanizing it and the space within which it functions. This doesn't keep me from admiring the work of those who can, however.

Besides this the figure allows my pictures a kind of encyclopedic inclusiveness of many almost incompatible things: personal conceits as well as universal ones, intellectual constructions as well as intuitive discoveries, order and clarity as well as Eros and violence. Some of these things may be unnatural to the art of painting but I am not yet convinced that a picture must grow naturally and exclusively like a flower, that it is not largely a synthetic object even if it can be made to look inevitable.

James McGarrell, Portland, Oregon, 1959

James McGarrell, the youngest painter in this exhibition, is indeed young enough to show the influence of other artists represented here without any detriment to his own work, which reveals extraordinary individuality.

McGarrell's world is an eccentric and irrational one. There is an uncanny, almost a hallucinatory quality to his paintings. A picture like *Bathers* (page 104) seems influenced by Lebrun, especially in the limbs of the figures, but the effect —the strange and haunting quality—is more closely akin to Bacon. The painting appears innocent enough at first glance, but then the deep hollow between hip and thigh of the large kneeling man becomes obsessive, as does the shadow—more that of a dog than of a man. The group seems to be participating in a weird, esoteric ritual, understood only by themselves and excluding the uninitiated, though its disquieting enigma continues to haunt the spectator.

And what is the meaning of *Equinox* (opposite) with its surrealist jungle of flame-like forms and its distorted figure of undetermined sex? Is it merely out of focus and will we understand it if we look at it more intensely? Will the violent storm inaugurate a comprehensible change; are we to witness the necromantic instant in which this painful and unnatural alteration occurs? Is that why the colors, belonging neither to summer nor to winter, are so outlandishly tinted? Again the spell which the artist is able to cast persists in the mind and

McGarrell: *Equinox*. 1956. Oil on canvas, 41 × 47″. Collection Wright Ludington, Santa Barbara

eye of the viewer. In the same way one wonders about both the psychological and the spatial relationships of the seated man with his long arms and the nude reclining woman in *Rest in Air* (page 105). McGarrell's dream world, in which logic has no place and our associations betray us, has its own mystery and takes us back to de Chirico's silent *Uncertainties of the Poet*.

McGarrell: *Bathers*. 1956. Oil on canvas, 43¾ × 48″. Collection Sterling Holloway, Encino, California

McGarrell: *Rest in Air*. 1958. Oil on masonite, 48 × 59¼″. Frank Perls Gallery, Beverly Hills

JAN MÜLLER   1922-1958

In our age the artist cannot take flight from the rottenness of society to portray just the spirit of man. He has a responsibility toward that stench if any awareness and must try to reach the more social position in his ethical and moral evaluation of life. He should portray life, but as life of possibility not the refuge and well-being stimulated by acrobatics without content. He has to find a way to the closer relationship among things and has to become aware of man's multiple sensitiveness not just tied down to the string of an apron of one thing called purity in our age. But what is purity, perfection or a multitude of ideas?

The artist has a responsibility toward that stench and cannot take flight to the Elysian Fields of the preciousness of perfection, the prism of the eye, but has to deal with matter complex. If not coming to the conclusion he must hint and try to portray and achieve the most of his inherent capacity instead of taking refuge into the laws pre-established for him, the prism of the eye of our age. Art is first and foremost content, actually any human manifestation with critical faculty goes away from the therapeutic element of the norm...

From a notebook 1956, Jan Muller

Müller: *The Heraldic Ground.* (1952-53). Oil on canvas, 14½ × 40½". Collection Mrs. Jan Muller, New York

Jan Müller was born in Hamburg in 1922. Persecuted by the Nazis, his family fled to Czechoslovakia and from there to Switzerland and on to Holland and to Vichy-France. In 1941 Muller came to the United States. During his enforced travels he had developed rheumatic fever. A heart operation in 1954 did not prove successful and fully aware of his condition he continued working without abatement. Between 1952 and 1958 he had eight one-man shows. On January 29, 1958, he died at the age of thirty-five.

Like Yves Tanguy, Müller was incited to paint by the experience of seeing a picture by de Chirico, but his work was to take an entirely different direction. He studied painting with Vaclav Vytlacil at the Art Students League and then with Hans Hofmann, both in New York and Provincetown from 1945 to 1951. Hofmann taught him a great deal about the intrinsic and dynamic quality of color, and between 1948 and 1950 Muller's paintings were made up of small and irregular squares of raw, mostly primary colors. Hofmann's tenet that color and form are sufficient onto themselves was at variance with the aim of a number of younger painters who were to join forces in the Hansa Gallery group, "representatives of a new generation of artists to whom figurative art was in a sense more revolutionary than abstraction and who pursued distinctly individual goals apart from the mainstream of Abstract Expressionism."[29]

In Jan Müller's own work the patches of color became slowly more than mere quilt work and specific figuration emerged as in *The Heraldic Ground* of 1953 (opposite) where the color areas are directed into a vigorous and exciting movement, which is emphasized by diagonals of the lances and culminates in the central group of a dark and a white horse confronting each other as if in battle. Although it was only in this country that he started to paint, the imagery which began to assert itself in Müller's work was peculiarly Northern and medieval. He drew inspiration from late Gothic altarpieces and made triptychs, folding panels and hanging pieces (page 108) where he combined a number of panels depicting all kinds of scenes reminiscent of the medieval bestiaries or gargoyles. Here are the horsemen, the mocking garish heads, women riding women, or the bacchanalian revels and abductions. He also turned his attention to great literary masterpieces and took for his paintings such themes as the gravedigger scene from *Hamlet*, the Walpurgis Night from *Faust*, or Jacob's Ladder from Genesis. In *Hamlet and Horatio* (page 110) the large vertical blue figure of Hamlet cradling the skull seems continued and buttressed by the smaller one of Horatio, painted in the same blue. Down below, the "grave-maker" digs "the house that will last till doomsday" with great vigor—an orange arrow shooting into the picture. Müller seemed to be preoccupied with

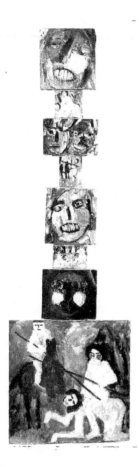

Müller: *Hanging Piece*. (1957). Oil on wood, 81" high.
Collection Horace Richter, New York

er: *Temptation of Saint Anthony.* (1957). Oil on canvas, 6′ 9″ × 10′ 2½″. Collection Mrs. Jan Müller, New York

Müller: *Hamlet and Horatio.* (1956). Oil on canvas, 50½ × 48½". Collection Richard Brown Baker, New York

the ancient contrast between the active and the contemplative life. The black and grey tree root in the background is like a living animal ready to rear up —a symbol of impending danger and death.

His paintings seemed to become larger in scale as they grew more complex and inventive in organization. His *Temptation of Saint Anthony* (page 109) was completed only a few months before his death. The flying figures in the upper left form the spikes of a wheel. In the center a devil is pulling a "soul" in the form of a rectangular, stiff and dead woman. Another wheel formation—as if the wheel were symbolic of the turbulence of the Temptation—occurs around the group on the right which reminds one of a church choir. In the center of this group is Saint Anthony, the man with a blue peaked hat and the book. His round, open, innocent face is in great contrast to the grimaces of his companions and the masks of the witches, demons and devils. He stands and observes a tumultuous drama in which human beings fall, fly, ride and are dragged in all directions. It is a Last Judgment as well as a Temptation, which, like a medieval mystery play, is enacted by masked folk. As we look at the two naked women riding the dragon on the lower left, and notice that its eyes and toe nails are painted red, we fully enter into the artist's spirit of grim humor.

STATEMENT BY MEYER SCHAPIRO

A year ago died Jan Muller, a young artist of thirty-five, one of the hopes of painting in America. He left an impressive body of work, intensely personal, outside the current of the familiar abstract styles, and marked throughout by a deep seriousness. From love of life, accepting a death which he knew to be very near, he composed an impassioned imagery of nakedness and joyous nature, of the innocent and the demonic, often in mythical terms: Saint Anthony and Faust. His landscapes and flowers are glowing ardent works that breathe his purity of spirit.[30]

Oliveira: *Standing Man with Stick*. 1959. Oil on canvas, 68¾ × 60¼". The Museum of Modern Art, New York, gift of Joseph H. Hirshhorn

NATHAN OLIVEIRA   born 1928

Every artist deals with his sense of reality; this reality is for him to determine, and involves a broad and varied range of expressive symbols.

The image of the human figure is the vehicle with which I can most positively relate.

My concern for the figure is primarily a formal one, growing out of the problems of painting itself. The implications are unconscious, for I have no desire to illustrate stories.

Nathan Oliveira, San Francisco, 1959

Nathan Oliveira states that his study with Max Beckmann at Mills College in the summer of 1950 was the most important experience of his formative years. Oliveira's two-dimensional figures are very different from the plastic volumes of Beckmann's bodies, and there is none of the German's complex iconography in his work. Both, however, are preoccupied with the relationship of the solid figure to the surrounding void, though Beckmann, in a need to protect himself "from the infinity of space," has filled it with a jumble of objects, while Oliveira welcomes the void emphatically.

Unlike most of his contemporaries, Oliveira is not concerned with activating the total surface of the picture plane; instead he places his figures solidly against a vacant and neutral background thus revealing his predilection for fifteenth-century Italian portraiture. His exhibition at the Alan Gallery in 1958 included two collages entitled *After Gentile Bellini*; and the painting *Standing Woman with Hat* (page 116) bears a strange resemblance to Piero della Francesca's *Portrait of the Duchess of Urbino*, not only because of stance and headdress but precisely because of the placement of the figure against the simple background. Her austere profile and inflexible doll's body are portrayed against the stunning blankness of space. There is a somewhat greater affinity between figure and ground in the slightly earlier *Seated Man with Object* (page 114) where the scratches and streaks link the man to the grey surface. These scratchmarks have, in fact, a directional flow, so that the figure appears to be traveling rapidly through space, while holding on to its chair and its black "object."

Oliveira experimented with the two-dimensional aspects of the figure by means of collages in which he pasted his subjects on sheets of paper, as if they

Oliveira: *Seated Man with Obje...*
Oil on canvas, 60 ×48". C...
Richard Brown Baker, New Y...

were suspended in mid-air. After this, even a subject presented in front view, like the *Man Walking* (opposite), is primarily experienced in terms of an outline shape. The large expanse of sky and the low horizon line make the dark form appear menacingly large as it looms at the front of the canvas.

Man Walking. (1958). Oil on
o × 48". Collection Joseph H:
1, New York

In the recent *Standing Man with Stick* (page 112) the paint has been so heavily
applied that it literally oozes from the surface, modeling the figure in low relief.
The rest of the canvas is a thinly painted neutral ground. The colors of the
figure itself are also of low intensity with certain areas suddenly emphasized by

Oliveira: *Standing Woman with Hat.* (1958). Oil on canvas, 40 × 30″. Collection Mr. and Mrs. Roy R. Neuberger, New York

jewel-bright splashes of pigment. The head is a dark brown oval, haunting in its effect through lack of specific features.

Oliveira's faceless figures seem as empty as the blank against which they are silhouetted. These personages travel through space which itself lacks both definition and limitation, and they appear as though they might vanish again in a moment. They are not so much the ghosts of humans as they are merely shapes, rapid, volatile emergences brought by the whim of the artist's brush, and bearing a deeper affinity to the soft void of his background than to the world of the viewer whose stance or shape they may casually assume.

EDUARDO PAOLOZZI   born 1924

Most of my work is made in wax, then taken to the foundry, either in London or Paris where artisans cast statues employing a technique only modified since the Egyptians.

The metamorphosis from orange coloured ephemeral wax originals to metal is accomplished by other hands.

The atmosphere in a foundry is of hard labour, patience, nervous tension and an unpretentious language.

No Romantic Ideas here concerning tools or work.

Several years ago at Welding school somewhere in Cricklewood, after happy weeks making constructions, cutting steel scraps for assembly, masquerading as a Worker with Luminous Ideas, the transfer of finished work to my largest crucible became inevitable.

To become a VICTIM *of technical methods or, equally frightening, a Prisoner of spontaneity and red-hot improvisation, seemed to me only equalled by assuming the role of a bronze lay figure maker, various permutations to order.*

A CERTAIN KIND OF ACCURACY BECAME NECESSARY AND THE NEED TO INCLUDE IRONY.

I was more interested in destroying certain formal ambiguities by using ready-mades of a mechanical nature than creating some kind of philosophy about machines, at the same time collaging words out of magazines. The inclusion of the phrase PLEASE LEAVE ME ALONE *on the back of St. Sebastian the Second, now resident in New York, is an arrow aimed at compassion.*

Eduardo Paolozzi, Thorpe-le-Soken, Essex, 1959

"Rational order in the technological world can be as fascinating as the fetishes of a Congo witch doctor,"[31] according to Paolozzi. What he creates, indeed, are necromantic fetishes of the technological world, automatons born of its fragmentation.

Eduardo Paolozzi was born in Edinburgh of Italian parents. He studied sculpture at the Slade School from 1944 to 1947 and then lived, studied and worked in Paris from 1947 until 1950. His metal constructions were exhibited at the Galerie Maeght and at the Réalitées Nouvelles. Convinced of the need to integrate sculpture with architecture, he did a series of steel and concrete fountains—abstract constructions of water and light—in London and Hamburg. But he soon tired of these eulogies on technology, and of designing for the service of industry, and began working toward a less utilitarian art, one which might be complete in itself.

During his stay in Paris, Paolozzi had grown close to Jean Dubuffet and became interested in *art brut*, and eventually was influenced by both. He admired Henri Michaud and also Giacometti. In Pompeii he found the petrified bodies of people and dogs haunting and hypnotic and somehow relevant to our time with its consciousness of death and destruction. He felt increasingly that the multi-evocative sculpture in the international exhibitions which relies almost entirely on spectator interpretations, was insufficient for him. During several years of introspection and experimentation he developed a more specific imagery to deal with man as part of a mechanized society, and began making powerful fetishes, encrusted with the scavenged rejects of technology.

His current, very personal technique was developed around 1956. Taking random objects, he presses them into slabs of clay, forming a negative impression into which he then pours liquid wax. When the wax solidifies with all the impressions on it, he has a storehouse of designs from which he can draw at will, assembling them into wax figures. These he sends off to the bronze foundry for unique castings.

Clockworks, wheels, locks, forks, parts of radios, phonographs, automobiles, bomb sights—all are used to create his rich surfaces, reminiscent of Chinese bronzes; at the same time they have the psychological effect of reminding the spectator of the nature of his civilization. The figures are static, columnar beings, pierced with gaping holes, yet retaining a basically closed, two-dimensional form. His St. Sebastians, and Japanese War Gods, his *Jason* and *Icarus* (pages 119, 120) and Cyclops are weird mythological heroes who have turned into pitiful robots—their armor corroded, their mechanism run down.

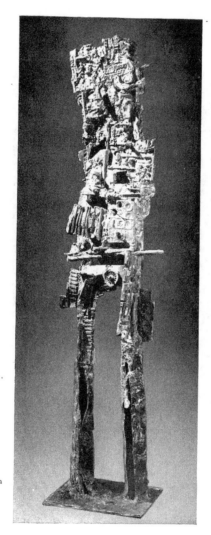

Paolozzi: *Jason*. (1956). Bronze, c. 66" high. The Museum
of Modern Art, New York. Purchase

Paolozzi: *Icarus, II*. 1957. Bronze, 60" high.
Betty Parsons Gallery, New York

Paolozzi: *Little King.* 1958. Bronze, 61" high.
Betty Parsons Gallery, New York

Paolozzi: *Very Large Head*. (1958). Bronze, 6′ high. Collection Mrs. H. Gates Lloyd, Washington, D.C.

JACKSON POLLOCK   1912-1956

The black and white paintings of 1951 are neglected in many assessments of Pollock. The ambiguous unification of disparate qualities in these works, which gives them their originality and their richness, also makes them difficult. In the more obviously astonishing inventions of the previous period, when *Autumn Rhythm*, *Out of the Web* and *Number 32*, *1950* appeared with their all-over energy, their chain-lightning and falling snow and sunlight, to apprehend one quality of a work, whether it was violence or lyricism, anxiety or nostalgia (as in *Lavender Mist*), was to be on the right track. Insight into one quality led onward to another until gradually the painting revealed itself in the history of one's responses: the violence of these works when they were first seen was only the sign of a subtlety which could not be immediately or easily assimilated. The conjunction of their qualities pictorially is scale, and it is achieved by that most aristocratic of contemporary artistic means: detail. But the black and white pictures of 1951 are another matter.

They are unsubtle and very complex. They are frontal assaults on imagery which had appeared in Pollock's work in the early 1940s and which, as if lurking in his subconscious through the intervening years, now come triumphantly to the fore. These paintings are the *Chants de Maldoror* of American art. Their compulsive figurative elements call forth associations which are totally false: we mistake the artist's subconscious for our own. Each work is a unique statement, simultaneously in terms of imagery and of esthetic stance. To fasten on any one quality is to misinterpret. *Number 3*, *1951* (page 124), is not an arabesque; *Number 6*, *1952* (page 127), has tenderness as its subject where a vicious spatial mutation, on first sight, seems to be occurring. As images they are counter to the theory of the collective unconscious; they are private and mysterious.

It is probably because they are not images at all, but ideographs from a subjective world we do not know. Just as *Maldoror* has a surface Byronism which leads us to feel familiar with it before we have known it sufficiently to experience its strangeness, so the semi-figurative aspect of this overt period of Pollock leads us to believe that we ascertain overt meanings. And we are quite wrong. Pollock did not "take up" the figure as a means of clearer communication. He employed it as one of the elements in an elaborate defense of his psyche, and through it he was able to make explicit and intransigent his conviction of the mystery of

123

Pollock: *No. 3, 1951.* Oil on canvas, 56¼ × 24″.
Collection Robert W. Ossorio, New York

Pollock: *Black and White Painting, 1951-52*. Oil on canvas, 35 × 31″. Collection Dr. and Mrs. Russel H. Patterson, Jr., New York

Pollock: *No. 23, 1951*. Oil on canvas. 58½ × 47". Collection Mrs. Martha Jackson, New York

Pollock: *No. 6, 1952*. Oil on canvas, 56 × 47″. Collection Mrs. Leo Castelli, New York

creativity. By this means he shows us the paltriness of recognitions, the vulgarity of obsessions, and the prodigal and lofty expenditure of his innermost resources which was so characteristic of him.

Alfonso Ossorio wrote, in his preface to the first exhibition of these works at the Betty Parsons Gallery, "His painting confronts us with a visual concept organically evolved from a belief in the unity that underlies the phenomena among which we live."[32] These phenomena include inner changes and the outward terror they produce. They also include, for Pollock, his own phenomenal work, a major *oeuvre* accomplished in barely fifteen years. The black and white paintings present the crisis of Pollock's evaluation of his own accomplishment. Unlike Franz Kline, who found in black and white the ultimate colors, Pollock here expounds no-color. It is as if, from 1947 to 1950, Pollock had so seduced and subdued the surface of the painting that it was now avaricious to absorb the essence of his life's action. As one looks, one does not know how long these signs, written large and plain, will last. Where before the canvas was a ground, a field, to be worked and developed, here it is a skin, the skin of an abyss which is contemplating its own nourishment. One of the dramas of these paintings is the intolerable conflict between an artistic intent of unerring articulateness and a medium which is seeking to devour its meaning. In the traditional sense, there is no surface, as there is no color. There is simply the hand of the artist, in mid-air, awaiting the confirmation of form. And these forms, which could have as well been painted on air, or on glass, like the *Number 29, 1950*, manage to refrain from disappearing, even though the complexity of motivation and demand is so extreme, because their own identity is his, and he is there and has the power to hold them. It is drawing, as so many of the great masters seem to tell us, that holds back the abyss.

Frank O'Hara

hier: *The Grasshopper.* (1946-55). Bronze, 21″ high.
lection Mr. and Mrs. Harold Kaye, Great Neck, New York

GERMAINE RICHIER 1904-1959

The human image has never been forgotten in the arts. The sculptor is not protected from the crises which have jolted modern art, but in sculpture, an art of slower evolution according to some, the disruptions are of a different nature. In some way it is sculpture that knew how to preserve the human face from these upheavals (in fact, today's sculptors do not renounce the making of busts). The face: that is to say, an entity, a whole of expressions and gestures brought into accord with the form.

This form, clearly, evolved to such a point that I would call it "hybrid." Whence come the dangers which threaten us through excess; and which are tempered through measure.

As an art of measure, the contemporary sculpture can and should erect and set up its forms, not in the pediments, but in front of monuments and public places. In order to make our times and the public understand the works of today, sculpture would have to take over the sites which—one asks why—have been denied it: large public squares, gardens, theaters, buildings, stadiums. As long as sculpture is not brought back into the "domain of man and woman," into the places common to humanity, its face will be as if it were disfigured.

129

Richier: *Hydra*. (1954). Bronze, 31″ high. Collection
Mr. and Mrs. Joseph R. Shapiro, Oak Park, Illinois

Richier: *Ogre*. (1951). Bronze, 30″ high. Allan Frumkin
Gallery, Chicago

*What characterizes sculpture, in my opinion, is the way in which it renounces the full,
solid form. Holes and perforations conduct like flashes of lightening into the material which
becomes organic and open, encircled from all sides, lit up in and through the hollows. A
form lives to the extent to which it does not withdraw from expression. And we decidedly
cannot conceal human expression in the drama of our time.*

Germaine Richier, Paris, 1959

Born near Arles, Germaine Richier came to Paris in 1925 and became a student of Bourdelle's about the time Giacometti left that atelier. Later she worked as Bourdelle's assistant. He himself had been chief assistant to Rodin for many years, and Richier seems to carry on the great master's comprehension of sculptural form: his animated, hollowed surfaces; his powerful masses; his expressive gestures and symbolist rhythm. Moreover for Richier the human figure remains the most important vehicle of expression, a means of interpreting the varieties of human experience. But Richier's world has become even more unquiet and menacing than the *Gates of Hell*. Rodin's figures are prisoners of an emotional and intellectual conflict, while Richier's, with their corroded surfaces, are often in a state of physical decay. Believing in the ancient struggle of the spirit against the flesh, Rodin still seems to leave hope for the ultimate victory of the spirit. Fifty years later Richier's figures have already been partially transmuted into insectile and vegetable matter.

Using the traditional techniques of the sculptor, she has cast in bronze a race of hydras, spiders, bats, praying mantises, six-headed horses and other ogres. Her effigies affect us by their strangeness, their existence on the frontier of human-ness. *The Grasshopper* (page 129), an enormous figure of which only the maquette is illustrated, seems to plead while threatening to pounce: an ambiguity which is far more human than animal. The ominous *Ogre* (opposite), with its swollen, gangrenous head; *Don Quixote of the Forest* (page 133), who has become a tree (or a tree which has become *Don Quixote*); the *Hydra* (opposite), whose once-human head is transformed into a threatening pitchfork or perhaps a petrified flower—these creatures with the odd grace of their hesitant stance and their romanticized ugliness initiate us into a mysterious world. A world, where to be ugly is somehow to appeal, and to be human is to partake at the same time of the qualities of animals, insects, plants, even objects—a kind of pantheism in which man is the spirit inhabiting all things.

Germaine Richier's sculpture, in contrast to that of her constructivist contemporaries, makes no reference to science. Yet hers is still a world of growth, change and decay. Like that of so many artists of this time, her work is concerned with transmutation, metamorphosis and organic interaction relating to the pattern unraveled by the physical scientists in their discovery of a continuous process in which the absolutes of time, space and matter have been abolished.

Richier: *The Grain.* (1955). Bronze, 59″ high.
Galerie Creuzevault, Paris

Don Quixote of the Forest. (1950-51).
7′ 9″ high. Walker Art Center, Minneapolis

THEODORE ROSZAK   born 1907

*"At first we cannot see beyond the path that leads downwards to 'dark and hateful things'
—but no light or beauty will ever come from the man who cannot bear this sight."*

C. G. Jung

*Because the total condition of man in the modern world is undergoing great change,
symbols that once acted as powerful agents in relating him to a sphere of ethical and moral
values have been steadily losing their meaning. Confronted by an historic and cultural
impasse, yet deeply concerned for the fate of his essential personality, man has no recourse
other than to recover the ground of his "Being."*

*The modern artist, acutely aware of the human predicament, re-creates proto-images that
cut across time. He mirrors the eternal spirit of man despite technocracy's chronic indifference
to his intuitive life, and wars against the current reduction of man's personality to a docile
and convenient cipher.*

*The new human content, as it appears in modern art is shaped organically out of an
evolution of forms that have a corresponding bearing upon historic necessity for us today.
It arises painfully, yet naturally, out of heaps of fragments and experiments that result
from decades of accumulated "visual ideas." It emerges out of a plethora of plastic elements
that belong entirely to our contemporary vocabulary, visually revealing bones, nerves and
senses as well as man's varied state of being. The life abundance suggested here, is of no
less importance than the inexhaustible store of shapes, volumes and space.*

*When considered in this light, sculpture emerges as a language of visual content in
space. The meaning of its forms evolves from the same organic source as the content within
forms—not as an "act" sufficient unto itself, nor as a repository for the "object" either
lost or found—but as an unequivocal statement charged to fulfill man's awakened sense
of his inner realities, upon whose threshhold of affirmation stands delineated—a new
image.*

Theodore Roszak, New York 1959

Roszak: *Skylark.* (1950-51). Steel, 8' 3" high. Pierre Matisse Gallery,

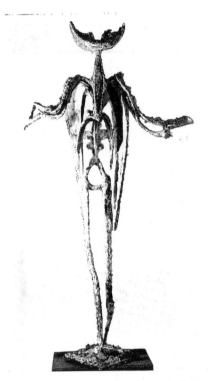

Roszak: *Rite of Passage*. (1952-53). Steel, silver-nickel and copper, 48" high. Pierre Matisse Gallery, New York

In the late Thirties and early Forties, Theodore Roszak, who had been a painter of cubist-romantic pictures, made constructions of brass, steel, wood and plastic. During a trip to Prague in 1929 and 1930 he had been tremendously impressed by the contrast of the medieval city and its modern surroundings. Recognizing that the machine was able to make clean and even beautiful shapes, he felt that art could and should be a functioning part of the new and better world which was to come about by synthesizing art, science and technology.[33] His friendship with Moholy-Nagy re-enforced his belief in constructivist laboratory experiments for the purpose of discovering the socio-biological relationships of man and modern society.

In time, however, Roszak found this approach disappointing. The theories of constructivism did not stand up against an industrial colossus with its mass values, its consumer surveys, its salesman's mentality. After teaching at the Design Laboratory in New York, he built airplanes and taught aircraft mechanics during the war. All the skills, all the extreme refinements of industrial precision, were used for purposes of devastation, and Roszak found himself becoming completely disillusioned with mechanization. He began to feel that art must look into nature for its inspiration, and that introspection might be more likely to produce meaningful results in his search for human values than would design for technology. He believes that the artist, alienated from society, can only acknowledge and respect this alienation.

His constructivist experiments had given him wide experience in the use of materials and techniques, as well as a broad understanding of the problems of form in space. Work with tools and machines, together with a rational and highly trained mind, has made it possible for him to proceed deliberately from drawings to blueprints to armatures before shaping and welding the steel of his finished sculptures. He does not rely on haphazard accidents.

While the techniques of constructivism were an aid, his sculptures since about 1945 are thoroughly different in form and feeling from his earlier works. They are pitted and gnarled where they used to be smooth and clean-cut. The interiors of his complex forms have become of uppermost importance. Agonized and convulsive forms organically determine a scorched exterior. This exterior is still sharp but no longer straightedged. Yet its hooks and thorns and prongs, in spite of their prickly appearance, are also beautifully textured from the rich brazing of copper, nickel and silver onto the steel.

The *Skylark* of 1950-51 (page 135) is an eight-foot skeleton surmounted by a bursting star, which could also be a maze, or a crown of thorns or the thyrsus carried by Dionysus and his satyrs. Indeed the figure seems "possessed." Roszak himself prefers to think of it as full of ambiguities with its upper part exultant and its lower half scorched and impotently exhausted. It is like a modern Icarus in whom flight and fall are expressed simultaneously. "It is this contrast," writes Paul Klee in his *Pedagogical Sketchbook*, "between power and prostration that implies the duality of human existence. Half winged-half imprisoned, this is man."[34]

If the *Skylark* is baroque in its thrusting dynamism, *Rite of Passage* of 1952-53 (page 136) seems more restrained. The very stylization and severe frontality recall ritual effigies. The figure moves in a slow dancing step, its arms coming down like feathered wings. The open bowl of the head resembles a crescent moon, and this crescent shape, bending downward or upward, gaining or waning, is repeated throughout the figure—a figure which is as majestic in its stance as it is vulnerable in its skeletal form.

In the *Surveyor* (page 140) Roszak develops the gesture, already important in the *Skylark* and *Rite of Passage*, so that it is the chief characteristic of the figure. The imperious stroke of the arm, a bow stretching up hugely before it reaches its straight vertical drop, is achieved with a complete absence of facial expression, as the gesture so often is in contemporary art. Yet the *Surveyor* has achieved mastery of his strange instrument, glittering like a jewel. Similar to an attribute of a medieval saint, this filigree of bright wire appears to have the importance of magic—an enigmatic power which is, however, controlled by the dominating gesture.

Suddenly, in the recent *Iron Throat* (opposite) Roszak dismisses the gesture as a major expressive means. This canine-human head is the portrait bust of a scream—agony, terror, warning. It is the iron cage of sound, its skull structure an intricate assemblage of metal webs and planes but yet altogether pared down, rejecting any gesticulating hand or striding foot in favor of the simple leaping throat, the reverberating hollows of the skull—an image of sound in clangorous flight.

Roszak: *Iron Throat*. (1959). Steel, 42″ high. Pierre Matisse Gallery, New York

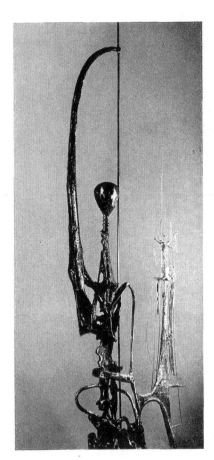

Roszak: *Surveyor.* 1959. Steel and silver-nickel,
7′ high, (detail). Pierre Matisse Gallery, New York

H. C. WESTERMANN   born 1922

H. C. Westermann can be seen as part of the Dada revival which has been
flourishing during the last decade and which seems to be as little confined to
any particular locality as was the original movement. The Dada groups which
sprang up in Zurich and New York during the First World War were a rebellion
against the lies of convention, against militarism and the suicide of the war. It
is hardly surprising that at a time when the means of mass communication have
made for a much greater conformity and when lunacy seems to have become
world policy, young artists conjure up a new kind of trenchant mockery.

But Westermann, who works in Chicago,[35] must also be seen as a highly
individualistic artist whose sardonic humor carries desperate implications. His
work lends itself to careful description. It states a message and can even be
considered literal in its forthright exposition. He makes objects—not sculpture—and, having set aside esthetic form, he creates unmistakable signs of
merciless intensity.

The Evil New War God (page 145), made of narrow brass and nickeled strips,
is a man in the shape of a blockhouse. Less whimsical than Paul Klee's graphic
similes, this is a grim image of war upon which our national motto has been
written with eloquent derision. Westermann served with the Marines during
the Second World War and again during the Korean War. Believing perhaps
in the power of the word, he scratched "Stop War" on the base of *The Mysterious
Yellow Mausoleum* (page 144). The purpose of this carefully carpentered structure is illusion. You can usually peep into Westermann's buildings through the
miniature windows and portholes, and as you explore the inside, you discover
steps which do not lead anywhere, a mirror contrived to make the viewer three-
eyed, a crucifix in the style of Mexican carvings, a black cat's head, a very old
newspaper clipping showing a dead soldier, a gallows, the sign of the skull and
bones surmounting the legs of a circus lady. Outside there is Brady's photograph
of Daniel Webster montaged upon Henry Clay's shoulders. All this is com-
manded by a tower with handless clock and graceless balcony and surmounted
by the deadpan baby-doll painted yellow with blue eyes.

The large *Memorial to the Idea of Man If He Was an Idea* (pages 142, 143) is his
most powerful creation. It is again a carefully worked box of laminated wood,
this time with wildly painted arms, vulgarly akimbo. Its castellated, monocular
head is topped by a toy globe, balanced on a pointed finger. A small man is

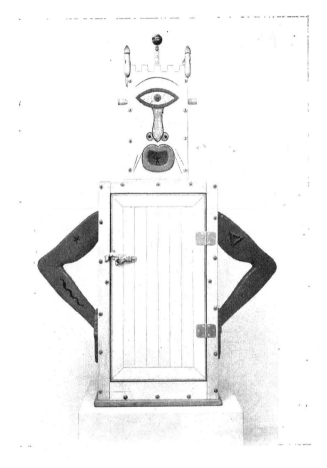

Westermann: *Memorial to the Idea of Man If He Was an Idea.* 1958. Wood and metal, 55″ high.
Collection Mr. and Mrs. Lewis Manilow, Chicago

Below: View with door open. Detail.

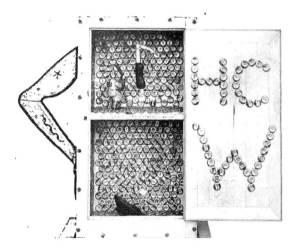

Westermann: *The Mysterious Yellow Mausoleu*
(1958). Wood, 49″ high. Collection Arthur
Neumann, Chicago

drawn on the glass between the heart-shaped lips. And a pigeon trough appears on the back: memorials to the idea of man may commemorate his vulnerability but they are still memorials and thus associated with pigeons.

The man's torso is a box with a door which opens to set us aghast. Here is a garish ocean of bottlecaps. The homeless Koreans are said to have built themselves houses out of empty beer cans left by the American soldiers. The jetsam of the civilization—the *objet trouvé*—became their homes. Here the bottlecaps serve as the ambiance for a headless baseball player, a helpless trapeze acrobat, a sinking ship. In one respect this is a self portrait: Westermann has been a circus acrobat and he served on the *U.S.S. Enterprise* during the war. The inscription to the "Mad Cabinetmaker" certainly applies with devilish accuracy. But this is also a succinct view of the world which has become a madhouse.

Westermann: *The Evil New War God.* (1958). Brass, partly chrome-plated, 17″ high. Collection Howard W. Lipman, New York

FRITZ WOTRUBA   born 1907

The human figure, now as much as ever, remains for me the starting point for my work, it
stands at the beginning and will stand at the end. As I see the theme, it carries no limitation
and I find it to be as topical as ever. It is not and never was a question whether to retain
the functional credibility in the creation of the figure. On the contrary, for me as a sculptor,
man in his physical reality is never as important as the fact that, because of his spiritual
and physical facets, he is the strongest stimulant among all existing objects and cannot be
replaced by anything else.

The metamorphosis and reduction may lead beyond recognition; but just as well to the
canon of the academy. Nevertheless, man himself is and remains the motive power for the
creative realization, even if nothing more of him is visible than a grimace.

Fritz Wotruba, Vienna, March 31, 1959

In physics and philosophy, in technology and communication, the elements of
change and motion underlie the concepts of our time. In one way or another,
a great many artists have attempted to cast these principles of transformation
and of a world in flux into visual form. Wotruba's sculpture, however, in its
search for permanence, harmony and structural density reveals itself as an
articulate protest against this emphasis on fluctuation. Time, motion have no
place in his ponderous and massive forms.

Born in Vienna, Fritz Wotruba is a truly rare phenomenon in the history of
art: an Austrian sculptor. At twenty he was carving torsos of classical proportions which, in fact, leaned rather heavily upon Greek models. In 1938, soon
after the Nazification of Austria, he went to live and work in Switzerland,
coming back to Vienna only in 1945 to become director of sculpture at the
Vienna Akademie der Bildenden Künste.

Since his return, he has dismissed the beauty and grace even of classical
sculpture as too-fleeting aspects of form, in favor of a more primitive severity.
His standing, lying or seated figures are compressed and compact, simplified
and static. The *Seated Figure* of 1948 (opposite)—a bronze cast from the original
limestone—has retained the rough-hewn quality of the carving. With its slab-
like body and cubed head, it recalls a pile of rocks found in a quarry or perhaps
at Stonehenge. Without resembling any particular primitive form, the figure

146

Wotruba: *Seated Figure ("Penseur").* (1948). Bronze, 32¼" high. Fine Arts Associates, New York

Wotruba: *Head.* (1954-55). Bronze, 16¼″ high. The Museum of Modern Art, New York, Blanchette Rockefeller Fund

has those universal qualities of inwardness and impersonal solidity found in faceless primeval idols. Wotruba does not like protuberances on his basic shapes. His *Head* of 1954-55 (above) is divested of all incidentals. It is a cylinder in which the large vertical gash and the triple furrows at right angles to it suffice to suggest a human head of barbaric strength and geometric precision. His more recent *Figure with Raised Arms* (opposite), carved directly in limestone, is a monumental variation on the theme of the cylinder. Cylindrical forms of various lengths and different positions off the vertical axis are played against each other to create a slow rhythm of verticality within the confines of the block. The stance and the proportion evoke feelings of dignity and strength. While this limestone figure may still recall classical art, it takes us back not to the pedimental sculpture at Olympir, but rather to the coarse-grained and unadorned drums of the ancient columns which stand among the pines in the sacred groves in the plain of the river Alpheus.

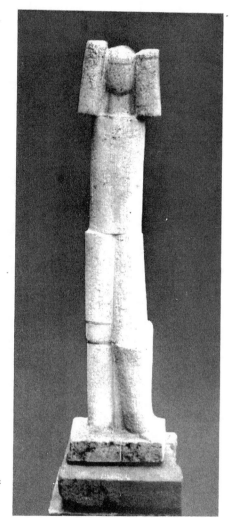

Wotruba: *Figure with Raised Arms.* (1956-57).
Limestone, 76⅜" high. Fine Arts Associates, New York

NOTES TO THE TEXT

1 Albert Camus, *The Rebel* (New York, Alfred A. Knopf, 1954) p. 46.

2 Guillaume Apollinaire, *The Cubist Painters* (New York, Wittenborn, Schultz, 1949) p. 22-23.

3 George Heard Hamilton, *Object and Image in Modern Art and Poetry* (New Haven, Yale University, 1954) [p. 5].

4 Francis Bacon [from a tribute to Matthew Smith, published in Smith retrospective exhibition catalogue, Tate Gallery, 1953], reprinted: *The New Decade*, (New York, Museum of Modern Art, 1955) p. 60-61.

5 The raw and spontaneous art of the insane, the deranged and the feeble-minded but also eccentric.

6 Kenneth Armitage: Statement by the artist, *The New Decade* (New York, The Museum of Modern Art, 1955) p. 57.

7 Herbert Read in *Art Since 1945* (New York, Harry N. Abrams, [1958]) p. 236.

8 Bacon's *Dog* of 1952 is closely related to a certain surrealist sequence at the end of Bunuel's film *The Young and the Damned* of 1950.

9 Compare Vincent van Gogh's *The Painter on the Road to Tarascon*, 1888. Kaiser Friedrich Museum, Magdeburg, Germany. Below.

10 Leonard Baskin: Introduction to catalogue on *Kollwitz* (Northampton, Smith College Museum of Art, 1958) p. 10.

11 From Reg Butler's description of the prize-winning model, from catalogue insert in *The Unknown Political Prisoner* (London, Tate Gallery, 1953).

12 Cosmo Campoli, in Patrick T. Malone and Peter Selz, "Is there a New Chicago School?" *Art News*, vol. 54, no. 6, October 1955, p. 37.

13 Paul Mills discusses the development of the new figurative painting in the Bay Area in *Contemporary Bay Area Figurative Painting*, a catalogue which accompanied the important exhibition he organized in September 1957 at the Oakland Art Museum. In addition to Park, Bischoff and Diebenkorn, a number of younger painters were included in the exhibition; among these William Brown, Bruce McGaw and Paul Wonner are of particular interest.

14 Jean Dubuffet, from a statement in the catalogue for his exhibition at the Pierre Matisse Gallery, New York, February—March, 1952.

15 Alberto Giacometti, $1 + 1 = 3...$, Trans/formation (New York) vol. 1, no. 3, 1952, p. 165.

16 Alberto Giacometti letter in *Alberto Giacometti* exhibition catalogue (New York, Pierre Matisse Gallery, 1948) p. 44.

17 Jean-Paul Sartre, "The Search for the Absolute" in *Alberto Giacometti* exhibition catalogue (New York, Pierre Matisse Gallery, 1948) p. 4.

18 Ibid. p. 6.

19 Richard Wilbur, from "Giacometti," in *Ceremony and Other Poems* (New York, Harcourt, Brace and Company, (n.d.) p. 51.

20 Ibid. p. 51.

21 René Char, *Recherche de la Base et du Sommet suivi de Pauvreté et Privilège* (Paris, Gallimard, 1955) p. 142.

22 Lawrence Alloway, introduction to exhibition catalogue on *Leon Golub* (Chicago, Allan Frumkin Gallery [1957]) [p. 4].

23 Compare *Dying Gaul*, Rome, Capitoline Museum. Right.

24 Willem de Kooning, "The Renaissance and Order," in *Trans/formation* (New York), vol. 1, no. 2, 1951, p. 86.

25 The *Crucifixion* triptych, which is the culmination of the series, was exhibited at the Museum of Modern Art in the Spring of 1951.

26 Rico Lebrun, "Notes by the Artist on the Crucifixion Theme" in *Rico Lebrun* exhibition catalogue (Los Angeles County Museum, 1950) p. 8.

27 Compare Francesco Traini: *The Three Quick and the Three Dead*, detail of the fresco *The Triumph of Death*, about 1350, in Pisa, Campo Santo. Right.

28 Rico Lebrun, letter to the author, dated April 19, 1959.

29 Martica Sawin, "Jan Muller: 1922-1958," *Arts* vol. 33 no. 5, February 1959, p. 39.

30 Foreword of the catalogue to a retrospective exhibition (New York, Hansa Gallery, December 1958).

31 Eduardo Paolozzi, "Notes from a lecture at the Institute of Contemporary Arts, 1958," *Uppercase*, London [1958], (n.p.).

32 *Jackson Pollock* (New York, Betty Parsons' Gallery, 1951).

33 Between 1937 and 1943 Roszak made many constructions such as the *Construction in White*. 1937. Wood, steel and plastic, 24" high. Owned by the artist. Right.

34 Paul Klee, *Pedagogical Sketch Book* (New York, Frederick A. Praeger, 1953) p. 54.

35 Franz Schulze, reviewing Westermann's first one-man show at the Frumkin Gallery, Chicago, sees him in the context of the "Chicago School." "...it is the most intensely private and compelling manner to emerge here in years and Westermann quite logically joins the Monster Roster (Campoli, Cohen, Golub, Halkin, Leaf, Rosofsky, et al) which has dominated Chicago art for a decade." *Art News*, vol. 57 no. 10, February 1959, p. 56.

Dying Gaul.

Traini: *The Triumph of Death*. Detail.

Roszak: *Construction in White*.

CATALOGUE OF THE EXHIBITION

In dimensions height precedes width, with the exception of some pieces of sculpture where the length is given. Dates enclosed in parentheses do not appear on the works of art.

KAREL APPEL. Dutch, born 1921

1   *The Condemned.* 1953. Oil on canvas, 55⅞ × 45¼″. Stedelijk v. Abbe Museum, Eindhoven, The Netherlands. Ill. p. 19.
2   *Person in Grey.* 1953. Oil on canvas, 46 × 35″. Martha Jackson Gallery, New York. Ill. p. 17.
3   *Portrait of Sandberg.* 1956. Oil on canvas, 51¼ × 31⅞″. Institute of Contemporary Art, Boston, Provisional Collection through Mr. and Mrs. Lester H. Dana. Ill. p. 21.
4   *Blue Nude.* 1957. Oil on canvas, 76¼ × 51¼″. Collection Philippe Dotremont, Brussels. Ill. p. 22.
5   *Count Basie.* 1957. Oil on canvas, 60 × 45″. Phoenix Art Museum, gift of Peter Rubel. Ill. p. 20.

KENNETH ARMITAGE. British, born 1916

6   *Seated Woman with Arms Raised.* (1953–57). Bronze, 41½″ high. Albright Art Gallery, Buffalo, gift of Seymour H. Knox. Ill. p. 26.
7   *The Seasons.* (1956). Bronze, 34″ high. Collection Mr. and Mrs. Charles Zadok, New York. Ill. p. 26.
8   *Model for Krefeld Monument.* (1956). Bronze, 13¼″ high. Collection Mr. and Mrs. Walter Ross, New York. Ill. p. 24.
9   *Model for Large Seated Group.* (1957). Bronze, 10″ high. Collection Mr. and Mrs. Maxime L. Hermanos, New York. Ill. p. 24.
10 *Diarchy.* (1957). Bronze, 68½″ high. Collection Mr. and Mrs. Arnold H. Maremont, Winnetka, Illinois. Ill. p. 25.

FRANCIS BACON. British, born 1910

11 *Man in a Blue Box.* (1949). Oil on canvas, 58 × 51″. Collection Mr. and Mrs. Joseph R. Shapiro, Oak Park, Illinois. Ill. p. 31.
12 *Study of a Figure in a Landscape.* (1952). Oil on canvas, 78 × 54″. Phillips Collection, Washington, D. C. Ill. p. 28.
13 *Study after Velasquez' Portrait of Pope Innocent X.* (1953). Oil on canvas, 60½ × 46½″. Collection Mr. and Mrs. William A. M. Burden, New York. Ill. p. 30.
14 *Study for Portrait of van Gogh, No. 1.* (1956). Oil on canvas, 60 × 46½″. Collection Mr. and Mrs. R. J. Sainsbury, London. Ill. p. 32.
15 *Study for Portrait of van Gogh, No. 3.* (1957). Oil on canvas, 78½ × 56½″. Collection Joseph H. Hirshhorn, New York. Ill. p. 33.

LEONARD BASKIN. American, born 1922

16 *Man with a Dead Bird.* (1954). Walnut, 64″ high. The Museum of Modern Art, New York, A. Conger Goodyear Fund. Ill. p. 34.
17 *Walking Man.* (1955). Oak, 17½″ high. Collection Dr. and Mrs. Malcolm W. Bick, Springfield, Mass. Ill. p. 38.
18 *Poet Laureate.* (1956). Bronze, 9″ high. Collection Mr. and Mrs. Roy R. Neuberger, New York. Ill. p. 36.
19 *Seated Man.* (1956). Bronze, 13½″ high. Collection Dr. and Mrs. Julius S. Held, New York. Ill. p. 38.
20 *The Great Dead Man.* (1956). Limestone, 5′ 10″ long. Owned by the artist. Ill. p. 37.

REG BUTLER. British, born 1913

21 *Woman.* (1949). Forged iron, 7′ 3″ high. The Tate Gallery, London. Ill. p. 40.
22 *The Unknown Political Prisoner (project for a monument).* (1951–53). Bronze with stone base, 17⅞″ high. The Museum of Modern Art, New York, Saidie A. May Fund. Ill. p. 42.
23 *Girl.* (1954–56). Bronze, 7′ 5″ high. Pierre Matisse Gallery, New York. Ill. p. 43.
24 *Figure in Space.* (1957–58). Bronze, 35¾″ high. Pierre Matisse Gallery, New York. Ill. p. 42.

COSMO CAMPOLI. American, born 1922

25 *Birth of Death.* (1950). Bronze, 33″ high. Allan Frumkin Gallery, Chicago. Ill. p. 46.
26 *Birth.* (1958). Bronze, 39″ high. Allan Frumkin Gallery, Chicago. Ill. p. 47.
27 *Mother and Child.* (1958). Marble, 7″ high. Allan Frumkin Gallery, Chicago. Ill. p. 48.
28 *Return of the Prodigal Son.* (1957–59). Plastic for bronze, 30″ high. Allan Frumkin Gallery, Chicago. Ill. p. 49.

CÉSAR (Baldaccini). French, born 1921

29 *Torso.* (1954). Welded iron, 30½″ high. Private collection, New York. Ill. p. 51.
30 *Nude of Saint-Denis, I.* (1956). Forged and welded iron, 36″ high. Collection Robert Elkon, New York. Ill. p. 52.
31 *Nude of Saint-Denis, IV.* (1957). Bronze, 24½″ high. The Hanover Gallery, London. Ill. p. 54.
32 *Winged Figure.* (c. 1957). Cast iron, 56″ long. Collection Mr. and Mrs. Richard K. Weil, St. Louis. (Exhibited in New York only.) Ill. p. 53.

RICHARD DIEBENKORN. American, born 1922

33 *Girl on a Terrace.* 1956. Oil on canvas, 71 × 66″. Collection Mr. and Mrs. Roy R. Neuberger, New York. Ill. p. 56.

34 *Girl with Cups.* 1957. Oil on canvas, 59 × 54″. Collection Richard Brown Baker, New York. Ill. p. 57.

35 *Man and Woman in a Large Room.* 1957. Oil on canvas, 71 × 63″. Collection Joseph H. Hirshhorn, New York. Ill. p. 58.

36 *Man and Woman, Seated.* (1958). Oil on canvas, 70½ × 83¾″. Mr. and Mrs. William Zeckendorf, Jr., New York. Ill. p. 59.

JEAN DUBUFFET. French, born 1901

37 *Childbirth.* 1944. Oil on canvas, 39⅜ × 31¾″. Collection Mr. and Mrs. Pierre Matisse, New York. Ill. p. 61.

38 *Archetypes.* (1945). Mixed media on canvas, 39¼ × 31¾″. Collection Leo Castelli, New York. Ill. p. 63.

39 *Dhotel with Yellow Teeth.* (1947). Mixed media on canvas, 45⅜ × 35″. Private collection, New York. Ill. p. 64.

40 "*Corps de dame – l'oursonne.*" (1950). Oil on canvas, 45¾ × 35″. Pierre Matisse Gallery, New York. Ill. p. 65.

41 *Woman with Furs.* 1954. Oil on canvas, 39½ × 32″. Collection Mr. and Mrs. Ralph F. Colin, New York. Ill. p. 66.

42 *Knight of Darkness.* (1954). Slag and clinkers, 35½″ high. Collection Mr. and Mrs. Albert A. List, New York. Ill. p. 66.

43 *The Dunce Cap* ("*La pointe au pitre*"). 1956. Assemblage on canvas, 57 × 45¾″. Pierre Matisse Gallery, New York. Ill. p. 67.

ALBERTO GIACOMETTI. Swiss, born 1901

44 *Man Pointing.* 1947. Bronze, 70½″ high. The Museum of Modern Art, New York, gift of Mrs. John D. Rockefeller, 3rd. Ill. p. 69, 72.

45 *Tall Figure.* (1947). Bronze, 6′ 7″ high. Private collection, New York. Ill. p. 72.

46 *Tall Figure.* (1949). Painted bronze, 65″ high. Collection Mr. and Mrs. James Thrall Soby, New Canaan, Connecticut. Ill. p. 72.

47 *City Square.* (1949). Bronze, 9⅛″ high × 25¼″ long. Mr. and Mrs. Pierre Matisse, New York. Ill. p. 71.

48 *Composition with Three Figures and a Head* (*The Sand*). (1950). Painted bronze, 22″ high. Collection Philip Johnson, New Canaan, Connecticut. Ill. p. 71.

49 *The Artist's Mother.* 1950. Oil on canvas, 34⅜ × 23½″. The Museum of Modern Art, New York, acquired through the Lillie P. Bliss Bequest. Ill. p. 74.

50 *Man Seated.* 1950. Oil on canvas, 31½ × 25½″. Collection Mr. and Mrs. Richard Deutsch, Greenwich, Connecticut. (Exhibited in New York only.) Ill. p. 74.

51 *Head of Diego.* (1954). Bronze, 26½″ high. Collection Mr. and Mrs. Sidney F. Brody, Los Angeles. (Exhibited in New York only.) Ill. p 75.

LEON GOLUB. American, born 1922

52 *Damaged Man.* (1955). Oil and lacquer on masonite, 48 × 36″. Allan Frumkin Gallery, Chicago. Ill. p. 77.

53 *Orestes.* (1956). Oil and lacquer on canvas, 82 × 42″. Collection Mr. and Mrs. Lewis Manilow, Chicago. Ill. p. 81.

54 *Colossal Head.* (1958). Oil and lacquer on canvas, 82⅛ × 48⅜″. Allan Frumkin Gallery, Chicago. Ill. p. 78.

55 *Horseman.* (1958). Oil and lacquer on canvas, 84 × 36″. Collection Mrs. Herbert S. Greenwald, Chicago. Ill. p. 80.

56 *Reclining Youth.* (1959). Oil and lacquer on canvas. 6′ 7″ × 13′ 9″. Mr. and Mrs. Lewis Manilow, Chicago. Ill. p. 82.

BALCOMB GREENE. American, born 1904

57 *Seated Woman.* (1954). Oil on canvas, 48 × 38″. Bertha Schaefer Gallery, New York. Ill. p. 84.

58 *Anguish.* (1956). Oil on canvas, 48 × 60″. Bertha Schaefer Gallery, New York. Ill. p. 87.

59 *Gertrude, II.* 1956–58. Oil on canvas, 64 × 49⅞″. Collection Mr. and Mrs. Joseph Weinstein, New York. Ill. p. 85.

WILLEM DE KOONING. American, born The Netherlands 1904.

60 *Woman.* (1950). Oil on canvas. 64 × 46″. Department of Art, The Woman's College of the University of North Carolina, Greensboro. Ill. p. 88.

61 *Woman, I.* (1950–52). Oil on canvas. 75⅞ × 58″. The Museum of Modern Art, New York. Purchase. Ill. p. 91.

62 *Figure in Landscape, No. 2.* (1951). Oil on canvas. 33¾ × 16½″. Collection Joseph H. Hirshhorn, New York. Ill. p. 90.

63 *Two Women's Torsos.* (1952). Pastel, 18¾ × 24″. The Art Institute of Chicago, the John H. Wrenn Fund. Ill. p. 94.

64 *Woman and Bicycle.* (1952–53). Oil on canvas. 76½ × 49″. Whitney Museum of American Art, New York. Ill. p. 93.

65 *Marilyn Monroe.* (1954). Oil on canvas, 50 × 30″. Collection Mr. and Mrs. Roy R. Neuberger, New York. Ill. p. 95.

RICO LEBRUN. American, born Italy 1900

66 *Buchenwald Pit.* (1955). Charcoal on canvas, 8′ 2″ × 6′ 8½″. Jacques Seligmann & Co., New York. Ill. p. 96.

67 *Study for Dachau Chamber.* 1958. Oil on canvas, 6′ 6½″ × 7′. Jacques Seligmann & Co., New York. Ill. p. 101.
68 *"Doble Disparate."* (1958). Casein and oil on board, 84 × 45½″. Owned by the artist. Ill. p. 98.

JAMES MCGARRELL. American, born 1930

69 *Bathers.* 1956. Oil on canvas, 43⅞ × 48″. Collection Sterling Holloway, Encino, California. Ill. p. 104.
70 *Equinox.* 1956. Oil on canvas, 41 × 47″. Collection Wright Ludington, Santa Barbara. Ill. p. 103.
71 *Rest in Air.* 1958. Oil on masonite, 48 × 59¾″. Frank Perls Gallery, Beverly Hills. Ill. p. 105.

JAN MÜLLER. American, born Germany. 1922-1958

72 *The Heraldic Ground.* (1952–53) Oil on canvas, 14½ × 40½″. Collection Mrs. Jan Muller, New York. Ill. p. 106.
73 *Hamlet and Horatio.* (1956). Oil on canvas, 50½ × 48½″. Collection Richard Brown Baker, New York. Ill. p. 110.
74 *Hanging Piece.* (1957). Oil on wood. Eight separate panels, 8:1′ high. Collection Horace Richter, New York. Ill. p. 108.
75 *Temptation of Saint Anthony.* (1957). Oil on canvas, 6′ 9″ × 10′ 2½″. Collection Mrs. Jan Muller, New York. Ill. p. 109.

NATHAN OLIVEIRA. American, born 1928

76 *Seated Man with Object.* 1957. Oil on canvas, 60 × 48″. Collection Richard Brown Baker, New York. Ill. p. 114.
77 *Standing Woman with Hat.* (1958). Oil on canvas, 40 × 30″. Collection Mr. and Mrs. Roy R. Neuberger, New York. Ill. p. 116.
78 *Man Walking.* (1958). Oil on canvas, 60 × 48″. Collection Joseph H. Hirshhorn, New York. Ill. p. 115.
79 *Standing Man with Stick.* 1959. Oil on canvas, 68½ × 60½″. The Museum of Modern Art, New York, gift of Joseph H. Hirshhorn. Ill. p. 112.

EDUARDO PAOLOZZI. British, born 1924

80 *Jason.* (1956). Bronze, c. 66″ high. The Museum of Modern Art, New York. Purchase. Ill. p. 119.
81 *Icarus, II.* 1957. Bronze, 60″ high. Betty Parsons Gallery, New York. Ill. p. 120.
82 *Little King.* 1958. Bronze, 61″ high. Betty Parsons Gallery, New York. Ill. p. 121.
83 *Very Large Head.* (1958). Bronze, 6′ high. Collection Mrs. H. Gates Lloyd, Washington, D. C. Ill. p. 122.

JACKSON POLLOCK. American. 1912-1956

84 *No. 3, 1951.* Oil on canvas, 56½ × 24″. Collection Robert W. Ossorio, New York. Ill. p. 124

85 *No. 23, 1951.* Oil on canvas, 58½ × 47″. Collection Mrs. Martha Jackson, New York. Ill. p. 126.
86 *Black and White Painting, 1951–52.* Oil on canvas, 35 × 31″. Collection Dr. and Mrs. Russel H. Patterson, Jr., New York. Ill. p. 125.
87 *No. 6, 1952.* Oil on canvas, 56 × 47″. Collection Mrs. Leo Castelli, New York. Ill. p. 127.

GERMAINE RICHIER. French, 1904–1959

88 *The Grasshopper.* (1946–55). Bronze, 21″ high. Collection Mr. and Mrs. Harold Kaye, Great Neck, New York. Ill. p. 129.
89 *Don Quixote of the Forest.* (1950–51). Bronze, 7′ 9″ high. Walker Art Center, Minneapolis. Ill. p. 133.
90 *Ogre.* (1951). Bronze, 30″ high. Allan Frumkin Gallery, Chicago. Ill. p. 130.
91 *Hydra.* (1954). Bronze, 31″ high. Collection Mr. and Mrs. Joseph R. Shapiro, Oak Park, Illinois. Ill. p. 130.
92 *The Grain.* (1955). Bronze, 59″ high. Galerie Creuzevault, Paris. Ill. p. 132.

THEODORE J. ROSZAK. American, born Poland 1907.

93 *Skylark.* (1950–51). Steel, 8′ 3″ high. Pierre Matisse Gallery, New York. Ill. p. 135.
94 *Rite of Passage.* (1952–53). Steel, silver-nickel and copper, 48″ high. Pierre Matisse Gallery, New York. Ill. p. 136.
95 *Surveyor.* 1959. Steel and silver-nickel, 7′ high. Pierre Matisse Gallery, New York. Ill. p. 140.
96 *Iron Throat.* (1959). Steel, 42″ high. Pierre Matisse Gallery, New York. Ill. p. 139.

H. C. WESTERMANN. American, born 1922

97 *The Mysterious Yellow Mausoleum.* (1958). Wood, 49″ high. Coll. Arthur J. Neumann, Chicago. Ill. p. 144.
98 *Memorial to the Idea of Man If He Was an Idea.* 1958. Wood and metal, 55″ high. Collection Mr. and Mrs. Lewis Manilow, Chicago. Ill. p. 142, 143.
99 *The Evil New War God.* (1958). Brass, partly chromeplated, 17″ high. Collection Howard W. Lipman, New York. Ill. p. 145.

FRITZ WOTRUBA. Austrian, born 1907

100 *Seated Figure ("Penseur").* (1948). Bronze, 32½″ high. Fine Arts Associates, New York. Ill. p. 147.
101 *Head.* (1954–55). Bronze, 16¾″ high. The Museum of Modern Art, New York, Blanchette Rockefeller Fund. Ill. p. 148.
102 *Figure with Raised Arms.* (1956–57). Limestone, 76½″ high. Fine Arts Associates, New York. Ill. p. 149.

SELECTED BIBLIOGRAPHY   by Ilse Falk

GENERAL REFERENCES

Art Since 1945. 374 p. ill. (col. pl.) New York, Abrams [1958].
  Texts on contemporary painting by M. Brion, W. Grohmann, Sam Hunter, H. Read and others. Includes references to Appel, Armitage, Bacon, Butler, César, Dubuffet, Giacometti, Paolozzi and Pollock.

ASHTON, DORE. Art [a column]. *Arts and Architecture* 1955 —current.
  New York correspondent regularly reviews current exhibitions.

BARR, ALFRED H., JR. Masters of modern art. 240. p. ill. (col. pl.) New York, Museum of Modern Art, 1954.
  Survey of major works and movements in the Museum collections. Bibliography.

GIEDION-WELCKER, CAROLA. Contemporary sculpture: an evolution in volume and space. 327 p. ill. New York, Wittenborn, 1955.
  Refers to Armitage, Butler, Paolozzi, Richier. Selective bibliography.

GREENBERG, CLEMENT. "American-type" painting. *Partisan Review* 22 no. 2: 179–196 Spring 1955.
  Refers to de Kooning, Pollock and others.

GUGGENHEIM, PEGGY, ed. Art of this century... 1910 to 1942. 156 p. ill. New York, Art of This Century, 1942.
  Catalogue of private collection with selected texts.

HESS, THOMAS B. Abstract painting: background and American phase. 164 p. ill. New York, Viking, 1951.
  Includes references to de Kooning, Greene and Pollock.

LAKE FOREST COLLEGE. The new Chicago decade, 1950–1960, an exhibition... at Henry C. Durand Art Institute... 36 p. ill. Lake Forest, Ill. [The College] 1959.
  Catalogue of exhibit of 14 artists including Cosmo Campoli. Introduction by Allan Frumkin.

NEW YORK. MUSEUM OF MODERN ART. The new American painting as shown in eight European countries 1958–1959. 96 p. ill. New York, Museum of Modern Art, 1959.
  Catalogue of circulating exhibit organized by the International Program. Foreword by René d'Harnoncourt, prefatory remarks: "As the critics saw it," introduction by Alfred H. Barr, Jr. Statements by the artists. Refers to de Kooning and Pollock. Also variant catalogues issued.

NEW YORK. MUSEUM OF MODERN ART. The new decade: 22 European painters and sculptors; edited by Andrew Carnduff Ritchie. 112 p. ill. New York, Museum of Modern Art, 1955.
  Exhibition catalogue. Refers to Appel, Armitage, Bacon, Butler, Dubuffet, Richier. Statements by the artists. Selected bibliography.

OAKLAND. ART MUSEUM. Contemporary Bay Area figurative painting. 24 p. plus ill. Oakland, 1957.
  Catalogue of exhibit with text by Paul Mills.

RITCHIE, ANDREW C. Sculpture of the twentieth century. 240 p. ill. New York, Museum of Modern Art, 1952.
  Includes references to Butler, Giacometti, Paolozzi and Roszak. Bibliography.

SCHAPIRO, MEYER. The younger American painters of today. *The Listener* 60 no. 1404: 146–147 Jan. 1956.
  Published on the occasion of the exhibition at the Tate Gallery: "Modern Art in the United States."

URBANA. UNIVERSITY OF ILLINOIS. COLLEGE OF FINE AND APPLIED ARTS. [Exhibitions of contemporary American painting and sculpture] 1948– current.
  Early catalogues refer to painting only. 1948–1952: later to painting and sculpture, 1953– current. Includes statements by the artists.

YALE UNIVERSITY ART GALLERY. Object and image in modern art and poetry. [34] p. ill. [New Haven. 1954].
  Exhibition catalogue with introduction by George Heard Hamilton. Refers to Armitage. Bacon. Giacometti. Greene, Pollock and Roszak.

KAREL APPEL

DOELMAN, C. Karel Appel: l'aventure de la sensation extasiée. *Quadrum* no. 3: 41–48 ill. Oct. 1957.
  English summary, p. 203.

GEORGE, WALDEMAR. Karel Appel, le Hollandais volant. *Prisme des Arts* no. 15: 41–43 ill. 1958.

ALLOWAY, LAWRENCE. Background to action: cobra notes. *Art News and Review* 9 no. 25: 2 ill. Jan. 4. 1958.
  Number 5 in a series of six articles on postwar painting. Brief bibliographies.

BURREY, SUZANNE. Karel Appel: Dutch muralist. *Architectural Record* 123 no. 1: 147–150 Jan. 1958.

KENNETH ARMITAGE

HERON, PATRICK. London [a column]. *Arts* (New York) 32 no. 3: 14–15 ill. Dec. 1957.
Review of Armitage exhibit at Gimpel Fils.

VENICE. ESPOSIZIONE BIENNALE. Catalogo. p. 269–278 ill. Venice, 1958.
29th biennale; includes sculpture and drawings, Kenneth Armitage; paintings and engravings, S. W. Hayter; paintings, William Scott; introduction by Herbert Read. Also separate catalogues issued by the British Council, London for circulating this exhibition in Europe.

FRANCIS BACON

MELVILLE, ROBERT. Francis Bacon. *Horizon* 20 no. 120–121: 419–423 ill. Dec. 1949–Jan. 1950.

HUNTER, SAM. Francis Bacon: the anatomy of horror. *Magazine of Art* 25 no. 1: 11–15 ill. Jan. 1952.

HOCTIN, LUCE. Francis Bacon et la hantise de l'homme. *XXe Siècle* (n.s.) no. 11: 53–55 ill. Dec. 1958.

LEONARD BASKIN

Graphic artists. *Art in America* 44 no. 1: 48–49 ill. Feb. 1956.
Statement by the artist.

WORCESTER, MASS. ART MUSEUM. Leonard Baskin, sculpture, drawings, woodcuts. 15 p. ill. Worcester, 1957.
Exhibition catalogue.

RODMAN, SELDEN. Conversations with artists. p. 169–177 ill. New York, Devin-Adair, 1957.
Reported interview.

RODMAN, SELDEN. The writer as collector. *Art in America* 46 no. 2: 29–31 Summer 1958.

REG BUTLER

MELVILLE, ROBERT. Personages in iron: work of Reg Butler. *Architectural Review* 108 no. 3: 147–151 ill. Sept. 1950.

GASSER, HANS ULRICH. Der englische Plastiker Reg Butler. *Werk* 38 no. 6: 189–192 ill. June 1951.

ALLOWAY, LAWRENCE. Britain's new iron age. *Art News* 52 no. 4: 18–20, 68–70 ill. June 1953.
Includes Butler and others.

LONDON. TATE GALLERY. The unknown political prisoner. [24] p. plus insert ill. London, Lund Humphries, 1953.
International sculpture competition sponsored by the Institute of Contemporary Art. Insert includes text by Butler on his prize-winning work.

HERON, PATRICK. The changing forms of art. p. 226–232 ill. London, Routledge & Kegan Paul, 1955.

MATISSE, PIERRE, GALLERY. Reg Butler, sculpture and drawings 1954 to 1958. [7] p. plus ill. New York, 1959.
Exhibition catalogue. Includes letter and poem by the artist.

COSMO CAMPOLI

MALONE, PATRICK T. and SELZ, PETER. Is there a new Chicago school? *Art News* 54 no. 6: 36–39, 58–59 ill. Oct. 1955.
Includes Campoli, Golub and others.

CÉSAR (Baldaccini)

COGNIAT, RAYMOND. César moderne Vulcain. *Prisme des Arts* no. 7: 8–9 ill. Dec. 1956.

ROUVE, PIERRE. No ides of March. *Art News and Review* 9 no. 22: 7 ill. Nov. 1957.
Review of exhibition at the Hanover Gallery.

HANOVER GALLERY. César. 19 p. ill. London, 1957.
Exhibition catalogue with introduction by John Russell.

RICHARD DIEBENKORN

CHIPP, HERSCHEL B. Diebenkorn paints a picture. *Art News* 56 no. 3: 44–47 ill. May 1957.

JOHNSON, ELLEN. Diebenkorn's "Woman by a Large Window." *Allen Memorial Art Museum Bulletin* (Oberlin) 16 no. 1: 19–23 ill. Fall 1958.

OAKLAND. ART MUSEUM. Contemporary Bay Area figurative painting. p. 10–13 ill. Oakland, 1957.
Text by Paul Mills.

JEAN DUBUFFET

PARROT, LOUIS. Jean Dubuffet. 20 p. plus ill. Paris, Pierre Seghers, 1944.
Issued on occasion of the first exhibition at the Galerie René Drouin.

TAPIÉ, MICHEL. Mirobolus, macadam & cie: hautespates de J. Dubuffet. 57 p. ill. Paris, Galerie René Drouin, 1946.

DUBUFFET, JEAN. Prospectus aux amateurs de tout genre. 154 p. Paris, Gallimard, 1946.

COMPAGNIE DE L'ART BRUT, PARIS. L'art brut préféré aux arts culturels. [52] p. ill. Paris, 1949.
Catalogue of exhibit organized by the Compagnie de L'Art Brut, shown at the Galerie René Drouin. Text by Jean Dubuffet.

MATISSE, PIERRE, GALLERY. Exhibition of paintings by Jean Dubuffet. 11 p. ill. New York, 1951.
Introduction by Michel Tapié with notes by the artist.

MATISSE, PIERRE, GALLERY. ...Jean Dubuffet, exhibition of paintings executed – 1950 and 1951. 15 p. ill. New York, 1952.
Includes statement by the artist.

LIMBOUR, GEORGES. ...L'art brut de Jean Dubuffet. 103 p. ill. New York, Pierre Matisse, 1953.
Includes notes by Dubuffet. Bibliography.

FITZSIMMONS, JAMES. Jean Dubuffet: a short introduction to his work. *Quadrum* no. 4: 27-50 ill. 1957.
Also published, with additional illustrations, as: Jean Dubuffet: brève introduction à son oeuvre. Brussels, Éditions de la Connaissance, 1958.

RAGON, MICHEL. Jean Dubuffet. *Cimaise* 5 no. 3: 11-22 ill. Jan.-Feb. 1958.
English translation: p. 7-9.

GUÉGUEN, PIERRE. Jean Dubuffet et le rachat de la matière. *Aujourd'hui* no. 20: 30-33 ill. Nov.-Dec. 1958.

VOLBOUDT, PIERRE. Les assemblages de Jean Dubuffet. 117 p. ill. Paris, XXe Siècle [&] F. Hazan, 1958.

ALBERTO GIACOMETTI

LEIRIS, MICHEL. Alberto Giacometti. *Documents* (Paris) 1 no. 4: 209-214 ill. Sept. 1929.

MATISSE, PIERRE, GALLERY. Alberto Giacometti, exhibition of sculptures, paintings, drawings. 47 p. ill. New York, 1948.
Introduction by J.-P. Sartre. Includes artist's letter in English and French.

LEIRIS, MICHEL. Thoughts around Alberto Giacometti. *Horizon* 19 no. 114: 111-117 ill. 1949.
Translated by Douglas Cooper. Revised for preface to Galerie Maeght catalogue, 1951.

MATISSE, PIERRE, GALLERY. Alberto Giacometti. 32 p. ill. New York, 1950.
Includes excerpts from his letter.

PONGE, FRANCIS. Réflexions sur les statuettes, figures et peintures d'Alberto Giacometti. *Cahiers d'Art* 26: 74-90 ill. 1951.

GIACOMETTI, ALBERTO. 1+1=3... [and] a letter from Giacometti. *Trans/formation* (New York) 1 no. 3: 165-167 1952.
Letter reprinted from Matisse Gallery catalogue, 1948.

SARTRE, JEAN-PAUL. Art and artist. p. 179-194 ill. Berkeley and Los Angeles University of California Press, 1956.
Translated by Warren Ramsey. Originally published in *Les Temps Modernes*, June 1954.

GENÉT, JEAN. L'atelier d'Alberto Giacometti. *Derrière le Miroir* no. 98: 1-26 plates June 1957.
Includes statements by the artist.

HESS, THOMAS B. Giacometti: the uses of adversity. *Art News* 57 no. 3: 34-35 plus ill. May 1958.

ASHTON, DORE. Art [a column]. *Arts and Architecture* 75 no. 7: 10, 31-33 July 1958.
Includes review of exhibit at Pierre Matisse Gallery, New York.

LEON GOLUB

GOLUB, LEON. A critique of abstract expressionism. *College Art Journal* 14 no. 2: 142-147 Winter 1955.

MALONE, PATRICK T. and SELZ, PETER. Is there a new Chicago school? *Art News* 54 no. 6: 36-39, 58-59 ill. Oct. 1955.

SELZ, PETER. A new imagery in American painting. *College Art Journal* 14 no. 4: 290-301 Summer 1956.

FRUMKIN, ALLAN, GALLERY. Leon Golub, paintings from 1956 and 1957. 11 p. ill. Chicago [1957].
Introduction by Lawrence Alloway.

BALCOMB GREENE

DE KOONING, ELAINE. Greene paints a picture. *Art News* 53 no. 3: 34-37, 48-51 ill. May 1954.

WILLEM DE KOONING

GREENBERG, CLEMENT. Art [a column]. *The Nation* 166 no. 17: 448 April 1948.
Reviews de Kooning exhibit at the Egan Gallery.

NEW YORK. MUSEUM OF MODERN ART. What abstract art means to me: statements by six American artists... 15 p. ill. New York, 1951.
Museum Bulletin 18, no. 3. Includes statement by de Kooning at a symposium on abstract art.

MOTHERWELL, ROBERT and REINHARDT, AD. eds. Modern artists in America: first series. p. 8-22 ill. New York, Wittenborn Schultz [1951].
"Artists sessions at studio 35" by Robert Goodnough.

DE KOONING, WILLEM. The Renaissance and order. *Trans/formation* (New York) 1 no. 2: 85-87 ill. 1951.

HESS, THOMAS B. De Kooning paints a picture. *Art News* 52 no. 1: 30–33, 64–67 ill. Mar. 1953.

FITZSIMMONS, JAMES. Art [a column]. *Arts and Architecture* 70 no. 5: 4, 6–10 ill. May 1953.
  Includes de Kooning at the Sidney Janis Gallery.

STEINBERG, LEO. Month in review [a column]. *Arts* (New York) 30 no. 2: 46–48 ill. Nov. 1955.
  Reviews de Kooning exhibit at the Martha Jackson Gallery.

ASHTON, DORE. Art [a column]. *Arts and Architecture* 72 no. 12: 10, 33–34 Dec. 1955.
  Reviews de Kooning at the Martha Jackson Gallery.

HESS, THOMAS B. Selecting from the flow of spring shows. *Art News* 55 no. 2: 25–27 ill. April 1956.
  Reviews de Kooning exhibition, the Sidney Janis Gallery.

HESS, THOMAS B. … Is today's artist with or against the past? *Art News* 57 no. 4: 26–29, 56–57. June 1958.
  Series of interviews which includes de Kooning.

RICO LEBRUN

LEBRUN, RICO. A letter from Rico Lebrun. *Chicago Art Institute Quarterly* 50: 18–20 ill. Feb. 1956.

LEBRUN, RICO. Art and artist. p. 68–88, ill. Berkely and Los Angeles, University of California Press, 1956.

RODMAN, SELDEN. The "Crucifixion" of Rico Lebrun. *Perspectives U.S.A.* no. 15: 69–81 ill. 1956.

LONGO, VINCENT. Exploration through collage: interview with Rico Lebrun. *Arts* (New York) 31 no. 2: 68–69 ill. Nov. 1956.

SELDIS, HENRY J. Artists of the West Coast. *Art in America* 44 no. 3: 37–40 ill. Fall 1956.
  Statement by the artist.

LANGSNER, JULES. Rico Lebrun, interim report. *Arts and Architecture* 74 no. 6: 20–21, 31 ill. June 1957.

LEBRUN, RICO. Rico Lebrun: drawings and paintings. (Fall release). 130 p. ill. Berkeley and Los Angeles, University of California Press, 1960.
  Introduction by James T. Soby.

JAN MÜLLER

SAWIN, MARTICA. Jan Muller: 1922–1958. *Arts* (New York) 33 no. 5: 38–45 ill. Feb. 1958.

EDUARDO PAOLOZZI

PAOLOZZI, EDUARDO. Notes from a lecture at the Institute of Contemporary Arts. *Uppercase* (London) [no. 1: 3–38] ill. 1958.

ALLOWAY, LAWRENCE. London chronicle. *Art International* 2 nos. 9–10: 36, 101 Dec. 1958–Jan. 1959.
  Reviews Paolozzi exhibition, Hanover Gallery.

MELVILLE, ROBERT. Eduardo Paolozzi. *Motif* (London) no. 2: 61–62 plus ill. Mar. 1959.

RODITI, EDOUARD. Interview with Eduardo Paolozzi. *Arts* (New York) 33 no. 8: 42–47 ill. May 1959.

JACKSON POLLOCK

POLLOCK, JACKSON. Jackson Pollock [a questionnaire]. *Arts and Architecture* 61 no. 2: 14 Feb. 1944.
  Translated into Italian in *I 4 Soli* 4 no. 1: 11 Jan.-Feb. 1957.

GREENBERG, CLEMENT. The present prospects of American painting and sculpture. *Horizon* 16 no. 93–94: 20–30 Oct. 1947.
  Includes Jackson Pollock.

POLLOCK, JACKSON. My painting. *Possibilities* (New York) 1 no. 4: 78–83 ill. Winter 1947–48.
  Translated into Italian in *I 4 Soli* 4 no. 1: 11 Jan.-Feb. 1957.

PARKER, TYLER. Jackson Pollock: the infinite labyrinth. *Magazine of Art* 43 no. 3: 92–93 ill. Mar. 1950.

PARSONS, BETTY, GALLERY. Jackson Pollock, 1951. [17] p. ill. New York, 1951.
  Exhibition catalogue with introduction by Alfonso Ossorio. Reprinted in "15 Americans," New York, Museum of Modern Art, 1952.

GOODNOUGH, ROBERT. Pollock paints a picture. *Art News* 50 no. 3: 38–41 ill. May 1951.

GREENBERG, CLEMENT. "American-type" painting. *Partisan Review* 22 no. 2: 179–196 Spring 1955.

FRIEDMAN, B. H. Profile: Jackson Pollock. *Art in America* 43 no. 4: 49, 58–59 ill. Dec. 1955.

NEW YORK. MUSEUM OF MODERN ART. Jackson Pollock. 36 p. ill. New York, 1956.
  Exhibition catalogue. Text by Sam Hunter. Also issued as Museum Bulletin 24 no. 2 1956–57. Selected bibliography.

GERMAINE RICHIER

GASSER, MANUEL. Germaine Richier. *Werk* 33 no. 3: 69–77 ill. Mar. 1946.

LIMBOUR, GEORGES. Visite à un sculpteur: Germaine Richier. *Arts de France* no. 17–18: 51–58 ill. 1947.

MAEGHT, GALERIE, PARIS. Germaine Richier. 7 p. ill. Paris, 1948.
  Derrière le Miroir, no. 13. Texts by Ponge, Limbour, de Solier.

SOLIER, RENÉ DE. Germaine Richier. *Cahiers d'Art* 28: 123–129 ill. 1953.

FRUMKIN, ALLAN, GALLERY. The sculpture of Germaine Richier... [First American exhibition]. 12 p. ill. Chicago, 1954. Introduction by René de Solier and Francis Ponge.

GRENIER, JEAN. Germaine Richier, sculpteur du terrible. *L'Oeil* no. 9: 26–31 ill. Sept. 1955.
  Translated in *The Selective Eye*, New York, Reynal [1956].

PARIS. MUSÉE NATIONAL D'ART MODERNE. Germaine Richier. [Préface de Jean Cassou]. 13 p. plus ill. Paris, Éditions des Musées Nationaux, 1956.

MANDIARGUES, A. PIEYRE DE. L'humour cruel de Germaine Richier. *XXe Siècle* (n.s.) no. 8: 45–48 ill. Jan. 1957.

GUTH, PAUL. Encounter with Germaine Richier. *Yale French Studies* no. 19–20: 78–84 plus ill. Spring 1957–Winter 1958.

WALKER ART CENTER. Sculpture by Germaine Richier. [Preface by H. H. Arnason]. 12 p. ill. Minneapolis, 1958.

CREUZEVAULT, GALERIE. Germaine Richier. [Préface de Georges Limbour]. [28] p. ill. Paris, 1959.
  74 works, drawings; biography, list of exhibitions, collections, bibliography.

THEODORE ROSZAK

ROSZAK, THEODORE J. Some problems of modern sculpture. *Magazine of Art* 42 no. 2: 53–56 ill. Feb. 1949.

KRASNE, BELLE. A Theodore Roszak profile. *Art Digest* 27 no. 2: 9–18 Oct. 1952.
  Extensive quotations from the artist.

MINNEAPOLIS. WALKER ART CENTER. Theodore Roszak... 55 p. ill. Minneapolis, 1956.
  Exhibition catalogue, in collaboration with the Whitney Museum of American Art. Text by H. H. Arnason. Selected bibliography.

ROSZAK, THEODORE. In pursuit of an image. *Quadrum* no. 2: 49–60 ill. Nov. 1956.
  French summary: p. 211.

H. C. WESTERMANN

SCHULZE, FRANZ. Art news from Chicago. *Art News* 57 no. 10: 49, 56 ill. Feb. 1959.

FRUMKIN, ALLAN, GALLERY. H. C. Westermann, recent work. 10 p. ill. Chicago [1959].
  Catalogue with introduction by Dennis Adrian.

FRITZ WOTRUBA

SALIS, JEAN-R. DE. Fritz Wotruba. 31 p. ill. plus plates Zurich, Édition Graphis; Amstutz & Herdeg, 1948.
  Text in English, German, French.

HOFFMANN, WERNER. Neue Arbeiten von Fritz Wotruba. *Werk* 41 no. 2: 69–72 ill. Feb. 1954.

CANETTI, ELIAS. Fritz Wotruba. 63 p. ill. Vienna. Bruder Rosenbaum, 1955.
  - English text.

PHOTOGRAPH CREDITS

Alinari, Rome. No. 5997, p. 151 top; Victor Amato, Washington, p. 28; Oliver Baker, N.Y., pp. 17, 20, 38 right, 66 left, 67, 75, 88, 90, 94, 95, 115, 116,.125, 126, 129; Paul Bijtebier, Brussels, p. 22; Brassai, Paris, p. 132; Brogi, Rome, No. 2243, p. 151 lower left; Rudolph Burckhardt, N.Y., pp. 57, 58, 63, 66 right, 106, 127; Colten, N.Y., pp. 64, 65, 74 left; Martien Coppens, Eindhoven, p. 19; Gwil Evans, Portland, O., p. 105; David Farrell, Gloucester, England, pp. 119, 120; Richard Fish, Los Angeles, p. 98; Sandra Flett, London, pp. 24, 26 right; Lidbrooke, London, p. 26 left; Herbert Matter, N.Y., pp. 14, 69, 71, 72; Rheinisches Bildarchiv, Cologne, p. 23; Walter Rosenblum, p. 26; Courtesy City Art Museum of St. Louis, p. 53; Edwin Smith, London, p. 122; Soichi Sunami, N.Y., pp. 12, 13. 30. 34, 37 left, 51, 74 right, 91, 108, 110, 124, 148; Charles Swedlund, Chicago, pp. 142, 143, 144, 145; Marc Vaux, Paris, pp. 52, 54; Herbert Walden, Worcester, Mass., p. 38 left.

31266

Date Due

Due	Returned	Due	Returned
SEP 21 73		MAR 0 2 1992	MAR 0 3 1992
		APR 1 6 1992	APR 2 0 1992
	OVERNIGHT RESERVE	OCT 3 0 1992	
		FEB 2 5 1994 FEB 2 1 1994	
FEB 1984 (F)	MAY 0 8 1985	AUG 2 2 1994 AUG 0 4 1994	
DEC 2 3 1985	DEC 1 4 1989	SEP 1 5 1994	1994
JAN 2 4 1986	JAN 2 6 1986		
MAR 1 7 1986		OCT 0 9 1994	
MAY 0 9 1986		OCT 2 7 1994	
NOV 0 3 1988	NOV 2 5 1988	NOV 1 6 1994	
APR 2 1 1989		DEC 0 6 1994	
	FEB 2 1989	DEC 0 7 1994	
NOV 2 1 1989		AUG 0 7 1996 JUL 2 4 1996 APR 0 9 2003 MAR 2 0 2003	
JAN 0 9 1990			
MAR 0 6 1990			
MAY 1 1990			
JUL 0 2 1990			
AUG 3 0 1990			
OCT 3 0 1990			
	OCT 2 8 1990		
NOV 3 0 1990	NOV 2 7 1990		
JUL 0 1 1991	JUN 1 3 1991		

Printed in the USA
CPSIA information can be obtained
at www.ICGtesting.com
LVHW072327080524
779785LV00032B/866